Tanaka

PROFILES IN **POWER**

General Editor: Keith Robbins

Tanaka
The Making of Postwar Japan

James Babb

An imprint of **Pearson Education**

Harlow, England · London · New York · Reading, Massachusetts · San Francisco
Toronto · Don Mills, Ontario · Sydney · Tokyo · Singapore · Hong Kong · Seoul
Taipei · Cape Town · Madrid · Mexico City · Amsterdam · Munich · Paris · Milan

Pearson Education Limited
Edinburgh Gate
Harlow
Essex CM20 2JE
England

and Associated Companies around the world

Visit us on the World Wide Web at
www.pearsoneduc.com

First published in Great Britain in 2000

ISBN 0 582 38216 5 CSD
ISBN 0 582 38215 7 PPR

British Library Cataloguing-in-Publication Data
A catalogue record for this book can be obtained from the British Library

Library of Congress Cataloging-in-Publication Data
Babb, James.
    Tanaka and the making of postwar Japan / by James Babb.
        p. cm. -- (Profiles in power ; 37)
    Includes bibliographical references and index.
    ISBN 0-582-38216-5 (csd : alk. paper) -- ISBN 0-582-38215-7 (ppr : alk. paper)
    1. Tanaka, Kakuei, 1918- 2. Prime ministers--Japan--Biography. 3. Japan--Politics and
government--1945-1989. I. Title. II. Series.

    DS890.T29 B33 2001
    952.04'7'092--dc21
    [B]   00-061358

10 9 8 7 6 5 4 3 2 1
06 05 04 03 02 01

Typeset by 35 in 10/12pt Janson Text
Produced by Pearson Education Asia Pte Ltd
Printed in Singapore

. . . .

CONTENTS

CONTENTS

LIST OF TABLES

PREFACE

Despite Japan's important role in the world economy for at least the past three decades, few people know the name of key Japanese political or social figures. I must express my special thanks to Andrew MacLennan who took my initial enquiry seriously and enthusiastically pursued the idea of a study of a major Japanese politician. He and his colleagues soon recognised the value of such a biography. I am grateful for their willingness to go beyond common preconceptions of Japan and the Japanese.

The main themes were presented at the annual Japan Politics Group Colloquium at the University of Birmingham on 7 September 1999. I very much appreciated the enthusiastic feedback of all the participants. Professor Tim Gray, my colleague in the Department of Politics at the University of Newcastle, kindly read the manuscript and supplied not only corrections and helpful comments, but also much-needed encouragement. Professor Keith Robbins, the 'Profiles in Power' series editor, made useful suggestions and corrections which improved the quality of the final draft. Of course, any remaining errors or omissions are entirely my own.

Mention should also be made of my wife, Fumie, who was very forgiving of the ways in which this manuscript preoccupied me at a critical time in her adjustment to life in Newcastle.

I would like to dedicate this book to my mother, Doreen Babb. She has taught me much that informs the writing of this book. Besides, it is a dedication that Tanaka himself would understand and approve.

Note: In order to avoid confusion, Japanese names are given in Western order, both in the text and in the Guide to Further Reading. I have generally omitted any indication of long vowels from Japanese words and names, crucial to the correct pronunciation of Japanese, except where names had existing transliterations into a European alphabet which it seemed more logical to use.

CHRONOLOGY

May 1918	Born in Futada village, Niigata prefecture
March 1934	Leaves home for Tokyo to work for Baron Okochi
March 1937	Creates Kyoei Architectural Office
March 1938	Conscripted and joins the Mokioka Cavalry, Third Brigade
Nov. 1940	Hospitalised for a lung infection in Manchuria
Aug. 1941	Returns to Tokyo and establishes the Tanaka Architectural Office
March 1942	Marries Hana Sakamoto. Birth of son, Masaho, later the same year
Dec. 1943	Forms Tanaka Civil Engineering Corporation
Jan. 1944	Birth of daughter, Makiko
Feb. 1945	Sent to Korea to build a factory
Aug. 1945	War ends. Repatriated from Korea
Nov. 1945	Makes a large donation to the Progressive Party
April 1946	Fails to be elected in first postwar general election
April 1947	Elected as an MP in the second postwar general election
Aug. 1947	Death of son
Nov. 1947	Leaves Democratic Party over coal nationalisation
March 1948	Joins Liberal Party
Dec. 1948	Arrested for bribery over coal nationalisation
Jan. 1949	Re-elected as an MP despite starting campaign in gaol
Nov. 1950	Convicted of bribery
May 1950	Passage of his first private member's bill
Nov. 1950	Becomes president of the Nagaoka Railroad
June 1951	Found innocent of bribery on appeal

June 1952	Creates an electoral support organisation (*koenkai*) called the Etsuzankai
Sept. 1955	Suspected of impropriety as police search Nagaoka Railroad offices
Nov. 1955	Formation of the Liberal Democratic Party (LDP)
July 1957	Appointed to cabinet as posts and telecommunications minister
July 1961	Appointed chairman of the Political Affairs Research Council, one of the three top LDP posts
Oct. 1962	Appointed to cabinet as finance minister
Nov. 1964	Reappointed as finance minister
Dec. 1966	Resigns over 'Black Mist' scandals
Oct. 1967	Appointed chairman of the Urban Policy Commission
Nov. 1968	Appointed LDP party secretary, another top LDP post
Jan. 1970	Reappointed as LDP party secretary
June 1971	Resigns post of party secretary after LDP losses in Upper House election
May 1972	Forms his own faction (81 MPs)
June 1972	Publication of his book *Remodelling the Japanese Archipelago*
July 1972	Elected president of the LDP and becomes prime minister of Japan
Sept. 1972	Travels to People's Republic of China (PRC) and announces normalisation of diplomatic relations between Japan and the PRC
March 1973	Proposes legislation to reform electoral system
Oct. 1973	Start of Arab oil boycott leading to 'oil crisis'
July 1974	Resignation of LDP vice-president Takeo Miki over Tanaka's political ethics
Aug. 1974	US President Richard Nixon resigns over Watergate
Oct. 1974	Publication of *Bungei Shunju* article critical of his financial affairs titled 'A Study of Tanaka'
Dec. 1974	Resigns as prime minister
July 1976	Arrested for Foreign Exchange Law violations. Later rearrested on bribery charges in the Lockheed scandal
Jan. 1977	Pleads innocent on first day of Lockheed bribery trial

1978–83	Effectively has the deciding vote in selection of Japanese prime minister
Jan. 1983	Convicted of bribery in Lockheed scandal; given a four-year prison sentence but remains free during appeal
Feb. 1985	Suffers a severe stroke after protégé Takeshita moves to take control of faction which has reached its peak of 123 MPs
July 1987	Faction dissolves as 113 MPs join the new Takeshita faction
June 1993	LDP loses power for first time since 1955. Daughter Makiko elected as an MP in same district as Tanaka had previously represented
Dec. 1993	Dies

Chapter 1

HUMBLE BEGINNINGS

In December 1993, in the intensive care unit of Keio Hospital in Tokyo, a 75-year-old Japanese man was struggling for his life. Eight years earlier he had suffered a serious stroke from which he had never fully recovered and, in addition to a serious thyroid problem, he was now suffering from diabetes. His daughter, Makiko, had visited him on the 16th: 'Daddy, when you feel better, let's go for a drive.' 'Let's go, let's go,' he replied enthusiastically. The doctor asked him, 'What do you like?' In slurred speech, 'I like to ride in the car.'[1] The next morning started a typical Tokyo winter day – cold but crisp. When the doctor saw him in the morning, the man said he was sleepy. In the afternoon, however, a rare rainstorm swept into the city and the air hung heavy. The man's breathing became difficult and by four minutes past two in the afternoon he had died of pneumonia.

The man was no ordinary man. He had been influential in Japanese politics in the decades after World War II, and between 1972 and 1985 was without question the most powerful politician in Japan. Even after his illness in 1985, and after his death, his followers and his legacy continued to shape Japan. Earlier in 1993, his daughter had been elected to his seat in the Niigata Third District which he had held since 1947. After his death, she would become one of the most popular and outspoken politicians in Japan, continuing his influence in another form. She would also become the heiress to his substantial fortune estimated at 11.9 billion yen or nearly $100 million.[2]

This man, Kakuei Tanaka, was by no means common, but his story is crucial to understanding the rise of the common people in postwar Japan. Pre-war Japan was hierarchical and only fitfully democratic, but by the end of the war in 1945, the social order had collapsed and men like Tanaka rose to prominence in a way that was unthinkable before the war. Like many Japanese, he sought to rebuild his identity on the foundations of the past, and yet, much of what he did was new. After all, Japan had changed decisively. The country was more democratic, and with the aid of politicians such as Tanaka, policy was now focused on improving the economic and social standing of the average Japanese. Moreover, the collapse of the pre-war social order led in the end to an unprincipled pursuit of financial gain at the expense of sober assessment of possible consequences of unbridled economic growth. The story of Tanaka's life exemplifies this change from pre-war to postwar Japan. In addition, an exploration of Tanaka's role in shaping the postwar period is crucial to understanding Japan today.

It is impossible to ignore the pre-World War II past as it provided the starting point for Tanaka and all of postwar Japan. The greatest contrast between the two periods is between the hierarchy and social distinctions of pre-war Japan, and the relative equality and democracy of the postwar period. The hierarchy of pre-war Japan does still linger in many ways, not least in the levels of politeness in speech and behaviour which continue to typify Japan, but the breakdown of status distinctions and the rise of the commoner are part of an ongoing process which has taken place over the past two centuries as the legacy of feudal Japan has faded and a modern Japan has begun to emerge.

Moreover, the desire for democracy and economic security has led the Japanese to aspire to a 'good life' which is as Western as it is Japanese. Japan wholeheartedly adopted Western technology and techniques, and at the same time tried to hold on to a Japanese spirit. The result was that physical goods and processes led to the introduction of modern business enterprises, factories, newspapers, markets and ideas. This was true throughout Japan, and as time passes, it has become difficult to identify the pure elements of old Japan. This leads some Japanese nationalists to bemoan the loss of pre-war order and the rise of democracy, but it must be noted that the imperatives of domestic political and economic demands in Japan, more than any external pressures, have determined the nature of change in Japanese society, as the case of Tanaka clearly demonstrates.

A romantic view of the past persists, nonetheless. Even Tanaka explained Japanese behaviour by pointing to the legacy of 250 years of semi-feudal rule of the house of Tokugawa and the maintenance of hundreds of domains (*han*) ruled by powerful local lords (*daimyo*) who were often nearly autonomous and absolute in their power over commoners who were irrevocably tied to their lands or their vocations. Tanaka's autobiography starts by noting the historical background of his home village, in which the local lord ruled his feudal domain, like all others, by means of the samurai, who were primarily warriors at first but evolved into a class of high-level civil servants.[3] The power the samurai wielded over commoners is legendary: they had the right to use the long and short swords they wore as symbols of their status to inflict summary punishment, including death, on those who displeased them. Tanaka's home prefecture[4] of Niigata was the site of two such feudal domains, Echigo and Echizen, where the loyalty of the people to their local lords was unquestioned, as in all such regions. It was natural for Tanaka to use the symbolism of the 'Echi' element of the names of these domains to lend weight and tradition to his own constituency support organisation, the Etsuzan Association.

It would be a mistake, however, to overemphasise the continuity in the influence of feudal traditions. By the nineteenth century, large numbers of samurai and entire feudal domains were slipping into debt. This increased the influence of nominally inferior financier-merchants – officially commoners – who occasionally were able to marry their children into samurai status. In the same period, peasant uprisings became more frequent and severe. Thus, when Japan was thrown into crisis as a result of confrontation with the West in the mid-nineteenth century, the old feudal system easily collapsed. A political *coup d'état* against the Tokugawa regime in 1868 was called the Meiji Restoration because in theory it 'restored' the emperor as the supreme ruler of Japan and was named after the new Emperor Meiji. However, the breakdown of the old feudal order did not produce a new era of egalitarianism.

. . .

THE NEW ELITE OF PRE-WAR JAPAN

As the old hierarchy was destroyed, a new one was created in its place. The leaders of the Meiji Restoration copied the system of peerage from Great Britain, giving themselves the titles of 'count' and 'marquis' despite an often middling or low samurai status, and bestowing similar status on powerful merchant families allied to the new regime. In addition, special titles and privileges were given to the various branches of the Imperial family, which had fallen into obscurity in the Tokugawa period, and to former Tokugawa lords, who were given a place in the new status hierarchy as well. Wealthy merchants, landlords and senior government officials constituted a new elite which grew in influence to occupy a central place in the pre-war regime.

Two domains, Satsuma (at the far end of Japan's southernmost island, Kyushu) and Choshu (at the southern tip of Japan's main island, Honshu), dominated both the overthrow of the Tokugawa regime and the Meiji state formed immediately afterward. At the same time as providing themselves and their supporters with new posts and titles, the Satsuma and Choshu elite – often known as the Meiji oligarchs – modernised Japan by abolishing the old domains, stripping the samurai of their swords and their status, and pensioning off lords and samurai alike in the process of creating a modern centralised state. In addition, the new regime also allowed commoners (i.e. non-samurai) to become public officials as well as soldiers and officers in Japan's modern army and navy.

This process of substituting one form of hierarchy for another did not go unchallenged, however. The early opposition to the Meiji oligarchy arose from disgruntled former samurai. While attempts to restore the old order were easily put down by the new Meiji army, the opposition was most successful when it combined radical ideas favouring democracy drawn from Rousseau with demands for an aggressive foreign policy. These demands led to a series of violent protests known as the Movement for Liberty and Popular Rights (*Jiyu Minken Undo*). In order to appease the supporters of this movement, the Meiji government pursued a policy of war and expansion into Formosa and Korea at the turn of the twentieth century. The government also established an elected Lower House of parliament with limited powers as part of the 1890 Imperial Constitution, though officially the concession of the constitution was a 'gift' of the emperor to his people. The movement itself, however, was quickly repressed by the authorities.

Nonetheless, the first elections for the new parliament soon led to the formation of political parties, with the opposition continuing to carry the banner of the popular rights movement. The problem was, however, that MPs represented only the largest taxpayers, so the opposition spoke primarily on behalf of disgruntled landlords who bore the brunt of the tax burden. The Meiji oligarchy was able to keep this and other new opposition parties under control through a combination of policies which included selective repression, bribery and the formation of a government party. However, one of the most effective methods of reducing the power of the landlord-based parties was to lower the tax requirement for voting rights and enable more non-landlords, particularly wealthier merchants and urban tax-payers, to participate in politics. By 1926, full manhood suffrage was achieved, though landlords and wealthy merchants still dominated party politics at the local level in most districts.

It was also the 1920s which saw the demise of Meiji oligarchic control of the government as the narrow elite which had carried out the Meiji Restoration died of old age. Links to the old Satsuma and Choshu domains became less important as commoners recruited and promoted on merit began to rise to the highest levels of official-dom. This development was particularly significant in the case of the military. The death of the hardline Meiji oligarch Yamagata Aritomo in 1922 was symbolic not only of the demise of Choshu dominance of the Japanese army but of samurai dominance as well. Unfortunately, this led to a decline in discipline within the military when newly promoted officers became increasingly prone to inde-pendent action in the field and susceptible to right-wing nationalist ideas as the old regional loyalties and samurai values declined in importance.

As the 1920s came to an end, these military radicals opposed more and more openly the influence of political parties over gov-ernment. The parties seemed poised to replace the old Meiji elite, but in the eyes of many military officers political parties seemed to be hopelessly corrupt and eager to pursue policies which weakened the role of the military. In particular, Japan's special rights in China appeared to be threatened and Japanese national security was seem-ingly put at risk as party governments inadvertently encouraged Chinese nationalism with policies of non-confrontation. In addi-tion, party governments participated in the negotiation of disarma-ment agreements and reduced the military's budget.

By the early 1930s, junior officers in the field began to take action, including participation in attempted coups against party govern-ments and independent military initiatives in China. While the officers and their extremist right-wing allies insisted on their loyalty to the emperor and the nation, their targets were wealthy business and party leaders who represented the economic and political elite of Japan. The young military radicals sought to act on behalf of the common people. However, in the aftermath of a failed coup in 1936, these radicals, notably the 'imperial way' (*Kodoha*) faction, were suppressed by the 'control' (*Tosei*) faction of army conservatives. This control faction essentially protected the domestic Japanese elite, though it was even more aggressive internationally than the imperial way faction and effectively seized control of Japanese foreign and security policy in exchange for supporting the status quo.

The political vulnerability of the Japanese elite was not surprising given its small size. A *Fortune* magazine special issue on Japan in 1936 put the number of Japanese 'gentlemen' at a minuscule 0.4 per cent of Japanese families with an annual income *per family* of more than $3,000 a year – approximately 50,000 out of 13,500,000 families.[5] Moreover, the new elite had little credibility as the traditional elite in Japan. It was a new aristocracy based on wealth created as a result of the industrial development of Japan after World War I:

> The old feudal aristocracy of ancient bloodlines no longer makes much sense except in the lingering pride of certain of those lines. Some of the new gentlemen of Japan come from the old aristocracy, are descended from the upper levels of the feudal soldiery (samurai). But the new Japan is an industrial power, her greatest riches are industrial riches, and they have created what is very largely an industrial aristocracy. The current gentlemen of Japan are very largely industrial gentlemen. Or their heirs.[6]

Despite the reliance of this small elite on the military and the state to maintain order, it would be a mistake to identify it with a backward-looking nationalism. The ideal of the pre-war Japanese elite was a hybrid of Western and Japanese elements, but it was the Western aspects, especially in the most modern cities, which were loci of the public and visible accretions of elite status:

> Japanese gentlemen work (if they do work) and live in cities which are a mixture of East and West, as are their habits. They work in the most Westernized settings in those cities, inside classical marbles and at mahogany desks, with Western panelling on the walls and often Western-style portraits. But the maid who brings in the green tea which refreshes business conferences usually wears a kimono, and when the gentleman gets through for the day, and goes out into his pilastered hall and down the Otis elevator and out the burnished revolving doors to his Lincoln or Cadillac at the curb, he moves into a hybrid city.[7]

This extended to private life as well, with the homes of the Japanese elite including Western-style rooms and many preferring Western domestic customs. This was particularly true with drink, which included French wines and Scottish whiskys as well as domestically produced beer and *sake* (rice wine).[8] Indeed, elite status and an affluent lifestyle in Japan meant acquiring the best of Western culture and technology as much as the better things which Japan had to offer. This was increasingly imitated by local elites, particularly landlords and merchants.

. . .

TANAKA'S RURAL BACKGROUND

The Meiji Restoration which made possible the modernisation of Japan also had an impact on non-elites. Peasants were given title to their lands and restrictions were removed on the activities of petty manufacturers and merchants. Commoners were also permitted to adopt surnames and it is no coincidence that Tanaka's surname is the most common surname in Japan; it literally means 'middle of the field', so was the choice of many peasant families and is in fact more common in Japan than the surname Smith in Anglo-Saxon countries.

Peasants not only gained title to their land but could also lose it by falling into debt to wealthier neighbours or merchants. Craftsmen and merchants accustomed to feudal guild protection soon lost out to their more entrepreneurial rivals. Peasants, craftsmen and others who failed in the new environment also 'enjoyed' the new freedom of movement to join the new factories and casual labour markets in the towns and cities. Poor peasant families sold their daughters to textile factories and even into brothels. The textile factories were strict and the wages meagre but it was possible for the young women working there to send money to their parents or save a small sum of money for marriage. While a few Japanese gentlemen lived the good life, most Japanese were farmers who eked out an existence on a small plot of land.

The poorest areas of Japan were in the north of the main island of Honshu in its Tohoku (Northeast) region, but also in Tanaka's home in Niigata prefecture located just below Tohoku, and these supplied much of the labour to an industrialising Japan. In part it was the climate of these regions that limited economic opportunities, which had to be sought elsewhere. Niigata prefecture is located on the Sea of Japan side of Honshu where it is directly assaulted by the frozen Arctic winds sweeping in from Siberia. In winter, the snow piles up several metres high and peasants in the region frequently had to play the waiting game of determining at what point fear of the heavy snow crushing their roof justified their going out into the below-freezing weather to clear the roof.[9]

Tohoku and Niigata were primarily agricultural areas with poor tenants and a handful of wealthy landlords and rice merchants. The status of the peasant was low in the pre-war hierarchy, with poor tenants being forced off the road and into the mud when their landlord or his family passed.[10] Respected above all were the civil servants in the community, who were officially the servants of the emperor, theoretically there to help the common people as a by-product of their duties to the state. Similar status accrued to others connected to the central government in the aristocracy, business and politics who might also be approached by the poorer members of society to seek aid in times of need. Tanaka came from a small farming family which placed him toward the bottom of the social ladder.

The percentage of tenant farmers in Japan was high (about one-third) and most farmers rented some land. However, it would be a mistake to overemphasise tenancy. Most farmers did own a large proportion of the land they worked, and there was a large population of petty landlords. Moreover, the agricultural proletariat, often the rural standard-bearer of the left in Western Europe, was small in Japan. It was primarily the commercialisation of the economy, most dramatically during and after World War I, that had the greatest impact on tenants in Japanese farm communities.

Indeed, the Rice Riots of 1918, usually considered working-class protest, also involved farmers because they had become so dependent on the market that even they were affected by rice price inflation.[11] In fact, commercialisation forced tenants onto the market and away from traditional relationships, and sometimes led to the formation of tenant unions. Given the poverty and despair of Niigata, it comes as no surprise that it is one area of pre-war Japan which had a strong tenants' movement which emerged as a result of the Rice Riots of 1918, the year of Tanaka's birth.

Even so, it would be inaccurate to term Tanaka's home village a typical village, especially in the context of Niigata. Futada village was unusual, for reasons historical and economic. It had been located at the entrance to the residence of a minor local lord, Hansaemon

Umetsu, and as a result had some of the characteristics of a small castle town which was at the heart of the Tokugawa period feudal domains.[12] For example, it has more than a normal share of Buddhist temples for a village of its size. Also, the village had few major landowners, with most farmers owning modest plots or renting land from landlords not much wealthier than themselves, and as a consequence, the tenant union movement gained supporters much later in Futada compared to neighbouring areas of Niigata. In addition, the discovery of oil in the village during the 1920s led to most households benefiting financially from the oil wells placed in their fields. While life was not easy for the people of Futada village, it was better than that of their neighbours.

This relative wealth did not seem to help Tanaka's family, however. His mother worked long hours to keep the farm running while her husband, Tanaka's father, engaged in various unsuccessful entrepreneurial pursuits. Tanaka remembered that his mother was always up earlier than him and was always still at work when he went to sleep – an amazing feat considering that Tanaka himself needed few hours of sleep. Tanaka's mother is prominent in Tanaka's autobiography, especially the image of a hard-working woman whose advice to him is remembered lovingly if not always followed.[13]

Tanaka's father, on the other hand, plays a minor role in Tanaka's memoirs. He seems to have been an operator who dabbled in ill-fated ventures. He lost most of his money when an attempt to import Holstein cows into Japan ended in disaster, as did a fish farming scheme. He was left with three thoroughbred racehorses, and though he did win some races, he was often unlucky. Tanaka remembers one race in which his father staked a large amount of money, but the horse stumbled and damaged its leg. Not only had he lost all his money, but there were the entry fees and the costs of disposing of the horse which remained unpaid. After a telegram from his father asking for help, Tanaka was sent by his mother to a local merchant to borrow a fairly large sum of money to send to his father to extricate him from his predicament.

. . .

PRE-WAR PORK BARREL POLITICS

Tanaka's family had not always been so poor and unsuccessful, however. His grandfather owned a construction firm which had managed to gain a number of lucrative local public works contracts such as the building of local government offices and schools. It is inconceivable that these contracts were awarded without some sort of political connections, which implies not only business success but also a good head for politics. In pre-war Japanese politics, local notables made money and channelled benefits to their clients. Pre-war politicians used government funds to provide direct benefits to their constituencies, competing to bring railroad lines, dams and other major projects to their districts, but compared to their post-war counterparts who have engaged in similar practices, they took greater gambles on uncertain ventures which often ended in the bankruptcy of the politicians themselves, even if clients such as Tanaka's grandfather did gain occasionally from connections with such individuals.

The main uncertainty of the pre-war period was deciding which political party to back. Once a political party captured control of the government, it could easily distribute enough patronage to manufacture an electoral majority. Local notables, including landlords and merchants – the new local elites of pre-war Japan – were able to control large blocks of votes which they would then mobilise in favour of one candidate or another depending on the prospects for the candidate's party to gain control of the channels of official patronage. As a result, local notables frequently shifted parties, opportunistically supporting different parties in different elections. As Scalapino has pointed out, every election in pre-war Japan was won by the party in power at the time of the vote.[14] Control of government meant control of government resources which could be used to attract the support of opportunistic notables and voters.

Change in control of the government by parties, then, came about only when the non-elective elements of the state (the Meiji oligarchy[15] and/or high-level bureaucrats) sought to play one party against the other by inviting one or other of them to form a caretaker government, or when the non-elective elements conducted the election, often with the intention of aiding one party or the other. If a candidate guessed wrongly about the implications of national-level political intrigues and backed the wrong party, the consequences would be disastrous.

As a result, pre-war Japanese politics was not a lucrative occupation. A common saying in pre-war Japan was that 'a politician could lose even the wall around his well', to indicate that even the most necessary assets could be lost by engaging in politics. In the case of

Niigata, there was one pre-war politician, Kanichi Otake, who operated in the same constituency in which Tanaka was to be active in the postwar period. Otake spent a large amount of his own resources to assist his supporters, supplying them with rice and loans in times of need to an extent that his own house deteriorated as a consequence. He is quoted as saying: 'How can I be so petty as to worry about my house falling apart when the country is falling apart?'[16] In contrast, most postwar politicians, like Tanaka, who were regularly elected in the same way as Otake, became wealthy.

The two established conservative parties remained in power because they controlled government patronage and assisted their local constituents. The benefits of government largesse included the development of roads, railroads and public utilities, such as electric power and waterworks. Since pre-war Japan was poor, opportunities for gain from the judicious siting of a railroad station or road could produce significant advantages for influential constituents. For example, when a plan to create a bypass around the town of Nakanoshima was proposed, Otake successfully opposed the plan on behalf of local merchants who stood to lose if the bypass was created. Not only would the bypass take away business, but it would also become the main central government-maintained route, which would mean that local residents would be required to pay for the upkeep of the existing main street, including the onerous task of snow removal in the dead of winter. In the event, Otake managed to divert the road-building funds to finance the widening of the existing road and maintain its status as a national highway qualified to receive central government maintenance. It was not until the 1970s, when Tanaka was able to move the local Shinto shrine and straighten the road, that a bypass was created without any loss to the local residents.[17] Certainly, the scale and comprehensiveness of largesse of a wealthier postwar Japan far outstripped that of the modest if significant schemes of the pre-war period.

One other contrast with postwar politics was that the pre-war conservative parties made no systematic attempt to match socialist appeals to the workers, tenant farmers, or struggling small business owners who comprised a significant percentage of the electorate. To do so would have required them to confront the landlords and business interests who were heavily involved in their parties. In large part this was because landlords and business owners could depend on a repressive state to arrest 'trouble makers', though some moderate socialists were tolerated if they kept within the bounds of existing political practice. The barriers to organisation by the socialist left included direct state repression, and more subtle forms of obstruction on a private level as has been documented in one well-known case in Niigata prefecture itself.[18] As a result, political appeals to tenants over the heads of landlords, and organisation of strikes and other direct action, brought the full force of the authorities down on socialist activists, especially on the left wing of the movement.

. . .

SCHOOL, WORK AND THE MILITARY

For most rural Japanese, therefore, the state existed in only the most rudimentary form: the police, schools and the military. Pre-war education was compulsory only for the six years of elementary school. Tanaka showed himself to be an able student with a remarkable memory and an enthusiasm for learning which made him stand out from his fellow pupils. His teacher recommended that he should go on to middle school. The number of students who could attend middle school was exceedingly small even if it was the only way to prepare for university, another preserve of the elite. However, such further education cost money. Tanaka imagined that the burden on his mother would be too much so he determined to proceed only to higher elementary school – three years of further education for those not going on to high school and university. His goal was to get a job as soon as possible.[19]

Tanaka also toyed with the idea of joining the military – one of the few avenues of advancement for able children of poor farm families in pre-war Japan. His interest was triggered in part by the Manchurian Incident in 1932. The Manchurian Incident had awakened a wave of patriotism in Japan after Japanese forces stationed in Manchuria, in northern China, effectively took control of the area and put in place a puppet government. While the League of Nations and the other major powers condemned Japan's actions, most Japanese believed that they were not only protecting their own interests but also restoring order to a China which had been torn apart by competing armies of local warlords. The sense of isolation created by international criticism only reinforced Japanese nationalism. In the end, however, Tanaka's enthusiasm for the idea waned when his mother fell ill and he realised that military pay would not be enough to support her. He would get a job, help support her, and be available to assist her as she needed it.[20]

After graduating from higher elementary school in 1933, Tanaka first took a job moving soil and stones as part of a government programme of public works for disadvantaged areas, for which Niigata easily qualified. Men were paid 75 sen an hour and women 50 sen (100 sen = 1 yen). When Tanaka received his first pay packet, he was surprised to find that he had been paid only 50 sen, the same as a woman. He was so angry that he refused to go the next day. The foreman, who came to see Tanaka to find out what was wrong, suggested that Tanaka should become a foreman himself if he didn't like the pay. The only opening for a foreman, however, was at another construction office in neighbouring Kashiwazaki City and Tanaka, who had only just left school, would have to compete with 20 other applicants. Nonetheless, Tanaka applied and was hired. His application stood out – he had been studying the middle school curriculum on his own at home in his spare time and was a keen calligrapher, both of which came through clearly in his application.[21]

His outstanding ability soon caught the attention of others. An elderly official at a neighbouring village council office had mentioned Tanaka to the owner of a major firm in charge of construction of factories in Niigata.[22] The owner, Viscount Masatoshi Okochi, wanted Tanaka to join his firm in Tokyo where he would be able to work while attending architectural design school. With trepidation, Tanaka cautiously approached his mother with the idea of his going to Tokyo, but her enthusiasm for the idea removed all his doubts. He was seen off at the station by a group of friends, but he was upset that the local telephone exchange operator with whom he had been flirting for the past several months had not come to the station to see him off as she had promised. His disappointment was short-lived; he was greeted by her one station down the line for a private farewell he never forgot.

As he passed over the mountains from Niigata, the snow became less and less, and by the time the train reached Karuizawa – the playground of the elite – there was no snow on the ground at all. He would later own considerable property in the area, bought from the aristocratic Mito branch of the Tokugawa family. After several hours, he arrived at Ueno station in Tokyo and took a taxi to the accommodation which had been arranged for him. At the end of the journey, the taxi driver asked for 5 yen, all the money he had. He knew something was wrong and protested but the driver was quite willing to go to the nearest police box to sort out the dispute. After paying, he later realised that the driver had driven him around in circles and overcharged him. The following morning, he travelled to work by bus but could not understand the driver who spoke too quickly so he had to jump off the bus when he realised he had nearly missed his stop. The receptionist also spoke too quickly and so politely he found it difficult to follow. The difference in the pace of life in Tokyo and Niigata depressed him. He trudged back to his accommodation through a snowstorm (rare in Tokyo) thinking that Tokyo was a difficult place in which to live.[23] It was an experience which made him sympathetic to millions who similarly were forced to leave their rural villages and travel to the big cities to succeed.

Tanaka's approach to human relations also betrayed his rural origin. He was so awed by Viscount Okochi that out of respect he would not ride in the same crowded elevator as his boss. When one day Tanaka had entered the elevator and the viscount came in after him, he was so overwhelmed with emotion at this first-time encounter with his benefactor that nearly 30 years later it still brought tears to his eyes to think that he had finally met the man who gave him his big start.[24] It is unclear why Tanaka was so impressed by his employer. After all, the aristocracy of pre-war Japan had been artificially created by recruiting remnants of the old Tokugawa hierarchy, the newly elevated Imperial family and prominent members of the pre-war regime, in order to resemble the status distinctions of a European monarchy. It is more likely that Tanaka respected him not only for creating a successful construction firm, but also as a visionary who believed that the building of factories in villages throughout Japan could be a solution to economic deprivation. The viscount was a member of the elite who cared for the common people. Some of his ideas appeared later in Tanaka's vision for Japan which helped to bring Tanaka to power and shaped Japan for years afterward.[25]

While Tanaka worked in the viscount's company during the day and studied at architectural design school in the Kanda district of Tokyo in the evenings, the international and domestic political situation remained unstable. The League of Nations had created a commission to investigate claims that Japan had manufactured the Manchurian Incident as a pretext to seizing control of Manchukuo. However, even when the commission confirmed the worst fears of Japan's critics, the League of Nations seemed powerless to act.

Within Japan itself, the Manchurian Incident and the weak reaction of the other Powers placed the military and extreme right-wing opposition in a position of increased influence in politics. The right wing had for many years declared itself in opposition to corrupt political parties and their relationship to the business elite which, it was argued, had weakened Japan internally and externally. Within the military, some factions plotted to overthrow the political parties. Attempted *coups d'état* as well as threats of coups were characteristic of the atmosphere of Tokyo in the period when Tanaka was studying and working as an apprentice. It was in the aftermath of one such attempted military coup in February 1936 that the *Tosei* (control) faction of the military was given carte blanche to suppress military uprisings. While the threat of domestic unrest receded with the rise of the *Tosei* faction, this faction was even more aggressive in its foreign policy and by 1937 Japan was at war with China.

In 1938, Tanaka was called for a medical examination and found healthy. He was conscripted, and since he could ride well, he was put in the cavalry, to be precise, the Morioka Cavalry Third Brigade, 24th Regiment, First Company. At the time, Japan had troops stationed in its colonies of Formosa and Korea, but the bulk of its forces were fighting Nationalist and Communist forces in China. Tanaka was unlucky to be stationed on the Russian border where major skirmishes were occurring between the Japanese Imperial Army and Soviet troops, termed the Nomonhan Incident. Serious casualties were taken on both sides and Japanese forces were badly bloodied in the battles by Soviet forces fighting to avoid a two-front war.

As a result of the difficulties experienced in moving north against the Soviets, the Japanese army decided to concentrate on moving to the south toward the colonial areas of France in Indochina, the British Empire in Hong Kong, Malaysia and Singapore, and the oil-rich Dutch East Indies (now Indonesia). The Japanese government knew that this course of action would put Japan in direct conflict with the United States and devised the attack on Pearl Harbor in December 1941 as a pre-emptive strike to discourage the US from interfering. The decision to move south after being bloodied on the Sino-Soviet border led directly to the beginning of World War II in the Pacific and the fall of the Japanese Empire.

One year after the Nomonhan Incident ended, in November 1940, Tanaka suddenly fell seriously ill with tuberculosis and a dangerously high fever. He was so close to death that he was moved from Manchuria back to Japan. While he was in hospital, one of his younger sisters, Toshie, died of tuberculosis. Tanaka heard of her death as he fought for his own life, but his determination to live was great and he miraculously recovered even though the doctors had written him off as beyond hope. In October 1941, two months before the Japanese attack on Pearl Harbor, he was discharged from the hospital, excused from further military service and allowed to travel back to his home in Niigata.

. . .

THE PLAN OF THIS BOOK

How did a relatively uneducated, small construction company worker discharged from the military for serious illness become the most powerful and important politician in postwar Japan? There is no question that Tanaka had both ability and good fortune, but that would not have been enough to ensure his success in pre-war Japan. It was the destruction of the pre-war world by the war and its aftermath which made the rise of Tanaka possible. In addition, he had intelligence and affinity with the common people of Japan which allowed him to serve them and gain their loyalty. His skills were as effective as they were questionable, and his legacy is mixed, but as a symbol of and catalyst for the rise of a new Japan, he is without equal.

Chapter 2 describes Tanaka's rise as a result of the war and its aftermath, and reveals his early experiences with corruption and scandal which shaped his future behaviour. Tanaka was not alone in these experiences: they characterised the lives of virtually all of the most outstanding of the new men created in the 1940s. Chapter 3 shows how Tanaka's passion for policy and a democratic desire to help all of his constituents led him to master the Japanese policy-making process and rise to become the youngest ever cabinet member. His experiences with the rough and tumble of factional infighting in the ruling party also provided valuable experiences.

Chapter 4 describes Tanaka's career as a prominent politician occupying the top posts in the ruling party and government. He uses his position to solve problems – in the economy and in politics – but his use of money and his ways of enriching himself and his allies begin to reach an unprecedented scale. In Chapter 5, we see how Tanaka establishes a government which is the culmination of his political manoeuvres and policy initiatives. He achieves more than any Japanese prime minister before or since and makes some of the most dramatic and lasting changes in Japan's political economy.

Chapter 6 reveals how Tanaka's success also contained the seeds of his downfall. Economic problems and allegations of wrongdoing are exploited by his enemies to remove him from office. Once out of office, he continues to be a power behind the rise and fall of governments even after his arrest on bribery charges in the Lockheed scandal. It is not until his betrayal by his own faction members and his subsequent stroke in 1985 that he retires from politics. Finally, Chapter 7 shows how Tanaka's legacy continues in the key politicians he trained and the policy initiatives he began which continue to affect Japan at present. Tanaka made postwar Japan what it is today.

. . .

NOTES AND REFERENCES

1 Yoh Mizuki, *Tanaka Kakuei: Sono Kyozen to Kyoaku* [Kakuei Tanaka: His Greatness and Wickedness] (1998), pp. 331–2.

2 *Yomiuri Shimbun*, 27 Sept 1994.

3 Kakuei Tanaka, *Watakushi no Rirekisho* [My Curriculum Vitae] (1966), pp. 1–2.

4 A prefecture in Japan is similar to an English county or a US state in terms of its size in relation to the whole country, but historically there is much more subordination to the central government than in the case of a state in the US.

5 'Special Issue on Japan', *Fortune*, Sept 1936, pp. 63–4.

6 *Ibid*.

7 *Ibid.*, p. 60.

8 *Ibid.*, p. 59.

9 Niigata Nippo Hodobu, *Tanaka Kakuei: Rongu Guddobai* [Kakuei Tanaka: Long Goodbye] (Niigata, 1995), p. 83.

10 Ann Waswo, *Modern Japanese Society, 1868–1994* (Oxford, 1996), p. 66.

11 Michael Lewis, 'The 1918 Japanese Rural Rice Riot: Taxation Populaire and the Tenant-Landlord Riots', *Working Papers in Asian/Pacific Studies: Rural Social Protest in Twentieth Century China and Japan*, Asian/Pacific Studies Institute, Duke University (Durham, NC, 1986), pp. 30–55.

12 Tanaka, *Watakushi no Rirekisho*, p. 2.

13 *Ibid.*, pp. 44–5.

14 Robert Scalapino, 'Elections and Political Modernization in Pre-war Japan', in Robert Ward (ed.), *The Political Development of Modern Japan* (Princeton, NJ, 1968), p. 283.

15 The Meiji oligarch is the term used to describe elite samurai from out-lying domains who led the overthrow of the Tokugawa Shogunate (1603–1868). They continued to be active and powerful behind-the-scenes players well into the twentieth century.

16 Toru Hayano, *Tanaka Kakuei to 'Sengo' no Seishin* [Kakuei Tanaka and the 'Spirit' of Postwar Japan] (1995), p. 178.

17 *Ibid.*, p. 177.

18 Kenji Yamamuro, '1930 no Nendai ni okeru Seito Jiban no Henbo: Niigata San-ku no Baai' [Transformation of Party Constituencies in the 1930s: The Case of the Niigata Third District] in Nihon Seiji Gakkai (ed.), *Gendai Seiji ni okeru Chuo to Chiho* [Center and Region in Modern Japanese Politics] (1984).

19 Mizuki, *Tanaka Kakuei*, p. 25.

20 Tanaka, *Watakushi no Rirekisho*, pp. 88–92.

21 Mizuki, *Tanaka Kakuei*, pp. 26–7.

22 Tanaka, *Watakushi no Rirekisho*, p. 44.

23 *Ibid.*, pp. 50–3.

24 *Ibid.*, pp. 99–100.

25 Mizuki, *Tanaka Kakuei*, pp. 27–8.

Chapter 2

WAR, BUSINESS AND CORRUPTION

Upon his return from military service, Tanaka found that his father's business ventures had started finally to produce some returns, and though he had now lost two younger sisters due to illness, the two remaining younger sisters had grown and matured into fine young women. With all well at home, Tanaka returned almost immediately to work, relying on his past connections with Viscount Okochi's company, and set himself up as an independent architect after borrowing a room from Kipei Sakamoto, a building materials firm owner.

Tanaka's relationship with Sakamoto was important for a variety of reasons, but most immediately because he introduced Tanaka to his future wife. Sakamoto's only daughter had been married previously and had a child from a previous marriage, but he was eager to have her marry again. Tanaka willingly obliged even though she was eight years older than him and he probably could have attracted a better match than a divorced mother. He put it down to fate and the fact that she was a quiet person who could put up with his unusual character.

There may have been another motive as well which undermines the Tanaka myth of his success in setting up his own building design business at the age of 19 and rising to become president of a construction company by the age of 25. There is little evidence that Tanaka's first business was a success and it was only the death of his father-in-law that put him in control of a construction firm which became the springboard for his future activities.[1] His father-in-law's business, Sakamoto Construction, was a relatively large supplier of construction materials. Business was suspended for a while after

Sakamoto's death, but Tanaka continued to pay rent on the office and made use of the building materials.

At the time, building materials were in short supply. Japan had been on a war footing since the late 1930s, but 1940 saw the creation of total mobilisation for war and December 1941 marked the beginning of war with the West as a result of direct attacks on the US and the colonial assets of her European allies (the UK, France and the Netherlands). In 1941, all business required permission to operate and building materials were designated (along with most other raw materials) as controlled supplies. In 1942, the government forced smaller firms to merge with larger firms to make more efficient use of existing resources. The business of which Tanaka was caretaker was not only large enough to remain independent but also benefited from the absorption of a smaller company. As a result, Tanaka changed the name of the company to Tanaka Construction; he was now the owner of a firm of over 100 employees.

War contracts meant that business was booming for construction as well as for manufacturing industries, fuelled by government contracts for war production which provided entrepreneurs such as Tanaka with opportunities for advancement and changed the nature of the Japanese economy. As the historian John Dower has pointed out:

> The labour force in manufacturing and construction increased from 5.8 million in 1930 to 8.1 million in 1940 and 9.5 million in 1944, and this was accompanied by a dramatic alteration in percentage of workers employed in light and heavy industry. In 1930, only 27 per cent of the industrial work force was in heavy industry, this rose to 47 per cent in 1937 and 68 per cent in 1942.[2]

Of course, Allied bombing raids began in earnest in 1945 and did much damage to Japan's urban areas, but the damage was primarily to buildings and often left equipment or raw materials unscathed. Moreover, the experience gained by the workers created a massive pool of skilled labourers, many of whom would be employed in Japan's postwar factories. It is no surprise that by the end of the war Tanaka's firm had grown to employ 300–400 workers.

The war also changed the lives of farmers who felt its impact in a variety of ways. There was a freeze on tenant agreements and rents, which was welcomed even if it was implemented to maintain food production. Moreover, many farmers were able to do well during the war, not only in spite of, but because of, economic controls. With growing food shortages in the cities, urban middle-class families were forced to travel to the countryside to barter away their prized possessions in exchange for a small amount of rice and vegetables. At the same time, the government sponsored the creation of wartime agricultural associations, the *nogyokai*, and extended the agricultural co-operative system throughout Japan. While many were dominated by landlords and other influential members of the community, the proliferation of control associations gave rise to numerous local officials who had not existed before the war. It has been argued that this 'democratised' rural communities in Japan during the war.[3]

This levelling phenomenon, which occurred in Europe as well as Japan, was a result of the demands of total war. In wartime Britain, for example, government economic controls contributed to a similar levelling process. After 1940, austerity and government regulations led to changing mores which produced growing uniformity, and as the social pyramid was flattened, social mobility increased.[4] The difference in Japan was that the social pyramid completely collapsed as massive wartime destruction as well as dishonesty and starvation led to a flourishing black market at the end, and in the immediate aftermath, of the war.

Tanaka's first real fortune emerged from these circumstances. Toward the end of the war, most major firms were wary of taking on further government contracts out of fear of losing money as the air war on Japan intensified and the possibility of defeat loomed large. Thus, Tanaka probably gained a major government contract to build a munitions factory in Korea by default. However, just as he arrived in Korea with a large sum of money and precious building materials, the war ended. Tanaka claimed that he left the material behind and was only able to return to Japan because the roster of the ship repatriating women and children allowed him to board because they had mistakenly recorded his name as Kikue, a woman's name.

It is widely believed, however, based on circumstantial evidence, that Tanaka sold the building materials and used part of the proceeds to bribe the captain of the ship to allow six co-workers and himself to return to Japan. The main evidence in support of such a theory is the large sum of money Tanaka suddenly seemed to have immediately after the war and the fact that even after the mistake in the ship's boarding roster was discovered, he was still given priority over women and children to return to Japan.

The situation was hardly unique. Bribery on repatriation ships was widespread, and the wholesale plundering of military supplies fuelled a massive black market in Japan. When the Allied occupation ordered the Japanese military to demobilise immediately after assuming control of Japan, the government of the time led by Prime Minister Kantaro Suzuki pretended that the order applied only to munitions, and allowed the wholesale pillaging of other army supplies. A special directive on 20 August tried to prevent further shifting of supplies into private hands, but the Higashi-Kuni cabinet, which succeeded Suzuki, delayed action for eight days. One authoritative observer later described the consequences: 'Meanwhile, of course, vast quantities of food, clothing and material were hauled away. Much of this fell into the hands of big business men, neighbourhood bosses, speculators, and bosses backed by political parties which claimed a rake-off of the spoils. The full story is a sordid one of black-marketing, corruption, and fraud . . .'[5]

The entire situation was ripe for the emergence of a gangster culture, with which Tanaka was often later identified and in which he was particularly well positioned to operate. The core of Japanese gangster culture is the *oyabun/kobun* relationship. Construction was one area of activity which was conducive to the *oyabun* (father-like patron) system whereby a man would attach himself to a patron who would command the absolute loyalty of his follower in return for assistance. An *oyabun* could supply a building project, in a flexible manner, with tools, materials, skilled craftsmen and day labourers. In order to maintain a ready supply of men and resources, the *oyabun* acted as a protector, a father surrogate, providing food, shelter and other necessities in good times and bad. In return, labour, loyalty and obedience were provided by the *kobun* (child-like client).

The system, if not widespread, was frequently found in industries such as construction which relied on day labourers and short-term contracts. It was also found in the transport industry, particularly in shipping and ports. There are also well-documented cases of its presence in the coalfields of Kyushu and Hokkaido where *oyabun* arrangements were also used to supply labour to the mines, with miners hired by and working for individual *oyabun* foremen rather than directly for the mining company.[6]

After the war, the collapse of the government and destruction of the cities saw the extension of areas requiring a strong presence to organise economic activity. It created an environment prone to gangsterism which would create order out of the chaos. Demobilised soldiers and homeless men were willing and available to pledge loyalty in return for protection. Petty gamblers and street stall organisers suddenly found their skills for dealing with a world without legal authority in great demand. Added to the mix were violent gangs of extortionists and blackmailers who set up independent operations to earn a living in a devastated economy. The roots of postwar Japanese organised crime and its gangsters (*yakuza*) can be found in this period, and the gangsters adopted the *oyabun/kobun* terminology as their own.

Tanaka's personal style of politics, drawn from his construction industry background, was legitimised in this period. It was an approach to politics which was drawn from many sources, including the mythology of the masterless samurai (*ronin*), but it was largely a postwar creation in terms of its scale and the degree to which it reached up into the highest level of political life. This approach was peculiar to Tanaka and a handful of others at the national level (with more prevalence at the local level), even if some have tried to make it the standard for successful leadership later in the postwar period.

Tanaka's autobiography is full of stories of debts and obligations which he never forgot. Of course, this is not so strange because most Japanese would be familiar with the conception of *giri* and *on*, roughly translated as obligation and debt of gratitude, but few would take these ideas to the extremes that Tanaka did. This was clear in the way in which Tanaka gave out his money at the time. When Tanaka became an MP for the first time, in 1947, he started giving out money to his fellow MPs. One of these MPs, Kenzo Matsumura, recollects:

> I do not know why but Tanaka gave me money. I am sure it was about 30,000 yen. At the time this was a large amount of money. It was said that many people had received it. I had no reason to receive the money so I went to return it. Two well-known MPs did not return it but I did. That was decisive. Tanaka was a simple person. He distributed money and those who accepted it were his friends, but those who did not take were enemies. From then on it was always that way with him.[7]

. . .

THE IMPACT OF THE ALLIED OCCUPATION OF JAPAN

Given the role of the government in the war economy, the social and economic chaos in immediate postwar Japan obviously had serious political implications. The wartime regime had incorporated the main political parties, but politicians who had refused to participate had been ostracised and the extreme left imprisoned. When the Allied occupation began, the first tasks to be undertaken were demilitarisation and democratisation. The military was abolished and political prisoners were released from prison.

While it was an Allied occupation in name, it was dominated by the United States, and the effective ruler of Japan for most of the occupation period (1945–52) was US General Douglas MacArthur. At the same time, General MacArthur relied on the members of his staff to plan and execute reforms. In the early years of the occupation (1945–8), the liberals on MacArthur's staff were in control and pursued radical reform of Japan.

For example, the emperor was forced to renounce his divinity in January 1946. This was followed by an extensive purge of the Japanese elite. Between 1946 and 1947, approximately 180,000 persons who had held key positions in Japanese society and government were purged by the occupation and forced to retire from public life. The purges not only removed many major politicians from power, but they also effectively eliminated the pre-war elite in most major firms and allowed a new group of junior managers to rise to the top. The break-up of the major *zaibatsu* conglomerates in 1947 and 1948 abolished the old elite families' control of stockholding companies by confiscating their shares and selling them to the public.

Occupation-sponsored land reform also destroyed the landlord's dominance of the rural community. The percentage of tenant farmers fell from 26.7 per cent in August 1947 to 5.5 per cent by the end of 1948. New labour laws passed in 1946 and 1947 gave workers the right to form trade unions and bargain collectively as well as setting labour standards for wages, hours, holidays, etc.

The new Constitution, approved by a vote of the Japanese people in April 1947, provided for popular sovereignty with the emperor playing only a symbolic role, universal suffrage giving women the right to vote for the first time, and an elected bicameral legislature as the foundation of a parliamentary government. Political parties were to be central to postwar Japanese democracy.

It is true that old party elements tried to rehabilitate themselves and the wartime elements sought new legitimacy, but the initiative was taken by the opponents of the wartime regime and new politicians who could give a new face to old parties. Moreover, the purges and other changes to the Japanese political landscape gave ambitious individuals such as Tanaka new opportunities to join the political elite.

This can even be seen, for example, in the Progressive Party, which was a direct outgrowth of the wartime political associations that were at the centre of the corporatist Imperial Rule Assistance Association (*Taisei Yokusankai*) which dominated wartime politics. Initial candidates for the presidency of the Progressive Party, such as Fumimaro Konoe and Kazushige Ugaki, were tied to political positions closely associated with the wartime regime. These veteran politicians, however, were opposed by younger members of the Japanese legislature who sought a clean break with the pre-war past, and as a result, the position of party president was left vacant for a time.[8] Ultimately, there was a fight for the presidency of the Progressive Party between Ugaki and Chuji Machida, former Minseito president. The presidency eventually fell to Machida, who was then 84 years old. It is alleged that the reason Machida defeated Ugaki was that the former outdid the latter in the collection of funds.

After the war, those with the greatest amount of funds for political purposes were those who had benefited from the chaos of the collapse of the wartime regime. As a former member of the Occupation forces noted at the time: 'Black-marketeers provide a deep reservoir of campaign funds. Although no official campaign contribution list includes their gifts, it is from them that all major parties have been financed.'[9] Unsurprisingly, one of the sources for Machida's funds was Tanaka.[10] Tanaka's own autobiography relates how he was put in contact with Machida who urgently needed campaign funds to support his bid for the Progressive Party presidency. Tanaka gladly agreed.

Tanaka had been introduced to Machida by Tadao Ohasa, a major MP who had been an 'advisor' to Tanaka's company since 1943. It was obvious that Tanaka was savvy enough to maintain some connection to leading politicians. Ohasa even suggested that Tanaka might himself run as an MP. Tanaka's main concern is telling of his attitude toward politics: 'How much will it cost?' he asked, to which

Ohasa replied, 'Spend 150,000 yen, keep quiet and ride the band-wagon. You will certainly be elected.'[11] Based on these encouraging words, Tanaka ran as a Progressive Party official candidate in Niigata's third district.

It made sense that Tanaka would be attracted to the Progressive Party. He had gained from his involvement with government during the war, and represented a new breed of 'common man' compared to the landlord and business elite politicians elected before the war. Although the Progressive Party included many veteran politicians such as Machida, the bulk of the party was composed of and funded by politicians similar to Tanaka.

The Progressive Party dominated the Diet from the end of the war (August 1945), through the first modest Japanese-sponsored land reform, and up to the first postwar election held on 4 April 1946. However, this party was completely transformed by the Occupation purges of individuals who had been involved in the wartime regime. The purge of politicians on orders from the Allied occupation authorities directly focused on the 381 members of the wartime Japanese parliament who formed the core of the Progressive Party. Out of the Progressive Party's 274 founding members, only 14 were able to pass screening of applicants for candidacy in the first postwar election. New candidates such as Tanaka were desperately needed to give the party a new image.

However, the Progressives suffered a crushing defeat in the April 1946 election. The party fell from an overwhelming majority in the parliament to just under 24 per cent of the seats after the general election and Tanaka failed to capture a seat. On the other hand, the Liberal Party, led primarily by conservative opponents of the wartime regime, rose to nearly 32 per cent of the seats, with the newly emergent Socialist Party in third place at 20.6 per cent and the next largest category being unaffiliated politicians with 17.2 per cent of the seats. As the Liberal Party obtained the largest number of seats (though not a majority), they set out to form a government with the co-operation of the Progressive Party.

The Liberals, however, were ill-equipped to face the economic chaos and social unrest of the immediate postwar period. The economy had collapsed, while at the same time the massive increase in the number of workers in heavy industry and in government services strengthened and emboldened the labour movement and the political left.[12] The rise in tenant unrest, which had been suppressed by wartime conditions, suddenly exploded into widespread social unrest in rural Japan. Yoshida and the Liberal Party toyed with land reform, but were unable to overcome the opposition of landlords who constituted the backbone of the party. The Liberal Party also tried to reduce labour unrest by enticing the moderate right wing of the Socialist Party into their cabinet, but such attempts were unsuccessful.

As the Progressive Party was reorganised into the Democratic Party, it moved away from supporting the Liberals and toward the Socialists. The Occupation, too, began to see the Liberal Party as an obstacle to the smooth implementation of Japanese government policy. Occupation authorities effectively promised the Socialists a general election as a *quid pro quo* for General MacArthur's prohibition of the 1 February 1947 general strike, a strike aimed at toppling the Liberal Party cabinet. The promulgation of the postwar Japanese Constitution became the pretext on which the election was eventually called. The Democratic Party was officially inaugurated the same day the election was announced. Tanaka ran again for parliament with the Democrats.

The Liberals were soundly defeated in the 1947 general election while the Socialists and the Democrats made massive gains with many MPs in both parties elected to parliament for the first time. Tanaka was one of the new Democratic Party MPs who substantially altered the character of parliamentary politics. However, since no party had an overall majority, negotiations towards a coalition government involved all of the major and minor parties, with the important exception of the Communist Party. The most conservative segments of the Democratic Party remained opposed to the coalition, but were too weak to impose their will on the party as a whole. The Liberal Party joined the early negotiations in preparation for the coalition, but eventually refused to join the government.

As a result, the Socialist leader Katayama became Prime Minister, and his party captured the lion's share of the portfolios in the new cabinet but shared control of the government with the Democratic Party. Tanaka was now poised to be part of the new government and was given the relatively senior position of chairman of the Commerce Committee of the Lower House of parliament, unusual for a first-term MP, but not entirely strange given the dearth of experienced MPs and his connections with the party leadership.

The main policy concession made by the Democrats to the Socialists was support for Socialist plans for the nationalisation of coal and other essential industries which was inserted into the common coalition platform. Even though conservatives in the Democratic Party, Tanaka among them, were opposed to nationalisation, the mainstream of the party believed it was an acceptable price to pay for building the coalition excluding the left wing of the Socialists. Indeed, the left wing not only accepted their exclusion from the cabinet, but senior left-wing Socialist MPs even held a press conference at which they formally renounced any ties with the Communist Party in order to placate conservative party fears. The nationalisation policy concession was the least the conservatives could do in return.

In retrospect, the failures of the Socialist and Democratic Party coalition are most often emphasised, but there were also positive impacts which are too easily overlooked. In addition to strengthening labour union rights, the new government was more sympathetic to land reform – and indeed the bulk of land reform occurred while the Socialists were in government. Progress was also made on breaking up Japan's pre-war industrial conglomerates and providing subsidies to heavy industry. These were broadly popular policies which played a key role in shaping the social foundation of postwar Japanese democracy, and were not at all objectionable to a populist politician such as Tanaka (at least in the long run).

Nonetheless, the coalition was in trouble from the start due to labour movement unrest and growing dissatisfaction with continuing requisitioning and other controls on the economy. The latter in particular reflected widespread resistance to Socialist attempts to create a bureaucratically led, controlled economy. The coal nationalisation dispute was the key issue around which this opposition coalesced – with Tanaka playing a prominent role – and it ended in severe damage to the coalition government from which it never recovered.

. . .

COAL NATIONALISATION AND COALITION FRAGILITY

State control of coal was to be the first in a series of postwar Socialist nationalisation plans for key industries. Other industries raised as candidates for nationalisation were steel, fertilisers and financial services – exactly the same industries that were at the core of the priority production system, the government's policy of giving priority in the allocation of scarce economic resources to those industries that were essential to the economy as a whole. The first public announcement of Socialist nationalisation plans came in late 1946, though the concept was mentioned in the party's initial post-war policy platforms. In fact, it was the main ideological pillar of declared Socialist economic policy. The coal nationalisation plan was the only identifiably socialist policy that emerged from the four-party agreement which led to the formation of the cabinet. Even in the initial stages, however, resistance to the plan by the Liberal Party and some in the Democratic Party was clear. The Socialists had to prevail on this issue if only to indicate political control.

The legislation was first debated by the Cabinet Economic Deliberations Council (*Keizai Kakuryo Dondankai*) on 28 June 1947. However, the Democratic Party members of the cabinet opposed the initial plan because it called for state ownership.[13] Instead, a Democratic Party plan was also drawn up, and both plans were debated in mid-August, and a compromise proposal was agreed. Even so, opposition continued from within the Democratic Party.

Both economic controls and nationalisation were useful in rallying small business to the Liberal Party in opposition to the government: indeed, small mine operators played a significant role in opposing the nationalisation of the industry. Moreover, money and organisational help in support of their cause came from larger firms. Shigeyoshi Kiso, the main figure working against the Socialist plan, helped organise small- and medium-sized firms in opposition to the programme with the support of big business.[14] The small firms could take actions which larger firms could not because the larger firms would risk being accused of trying simply to maintain their control of the Japanese economy. Small mining interests were particularly notorious for their 'extralegal tactics,'[15] the most famous of which was the bribery of politicians. As Samuels delicately put it, 'It was widely rumoured that cautious large mining interests used smaller firms to distribute funds to politicians.'[16] These acts of blatant bribery constituted the first of several major postwar scandals. Numerous politicians were implicated, and court records of those tried for the crime provide insight into the ways in which big business money was channelled to Democratic Party politicians, including Tanaka.[17]

When the coal nationalisation bill finally came up for a vote in committee, it was actually defeated, with many Democratic Party members voting against the party position together with the opposition Liberal and Communist Parties. Even so, the bill was brought immediately to a vote on the floor of the Lower House, and was passed. The opposition was upset that they had been out-manoeuvred, but the final version of the legislation passed was hardly a victory for the Socialists either. State 'control' of the mines was to be only temporary (for three years) and the control itself was to be exercised by institutions dominated by mining interests, not by the central bureaucracy or democratically controlled boards. The law did contain some penalty provisions for coal mine owners who did not comply (though these were never enforced), but the main feature of the legislation was enhanced financing to increase coal production.

The political effect of the legislation was far greater than the economic effect. As a result of the animosity created over the fight to pass the bill, 18 members of the Democratic Party either quit the party or were expelled. In addition, the grassroots opposition to nationalisation which had either supported the Democratic Party, or at least been neutral, moved over into the Liberal Party camp.[18] Thus, the damage to the Democratic Party and to the coalition was extensive. This issue weakened the cabinet so that later shocks more easily brought it down. By early 1948, analysts began to suggest that the momentum was moving away from the centre parties to the Liberal and Communist Parties at the extremes.

Tanaka played a particularly prominent role in Democratic Party opposition to the coal nationalisation legislation, in part because of his key position as chairman of the Commerce Committee of the Lower House of parliament. However, his involvement in the issue went much deeper – so much so, in fact, that he was one of a number of Democratic Party politicians indicted on charges of accepting bribes in exchange for mobilising their party against the bill. Tanaka's involvement was a direct outgrowth of his attempt to expand his business on a national scale. At the time, the coal industry was one of a few select industries targeted by the government for priority production with subsidies and preferential treatment to promote those industries that were central to postwar Japanese recovery. Tanaka believed that he could benefit from the expansion of the coal industry by political connections with coal operators in Japan's southern island of Kyushu where many major coal operations were located.[19] The problem was that the main players with whom Tanaka became involved were at the centre of the coal legislation bribery scandal.

By the time the scandal broke, Tanaka had quit the Democratic Party and joined the Liberal Party. As a result of his and other similar defections, the Liberal Party changed its name to the Democratic Liberal Party. The Democratic Liberals soon replaced the unstable Socialist–Democratic coalition government in October 1948 and began acting as a caretaker government until an election date could be set. Tanaka had joined the new government as a political vice-minister in the Justice Department – a very high-profile job which was presumably his reward for defecting from the Democratic Party earlier in the year. Once the scandal broke, Tanaka was forced to resign. The public prosecutor's office requested his arrest but he could not be arrested due to his parliamentary immunity. It was only after his fellow MPs stripped him of his immunity that an arrest was made on 13 December 1948.

Meanwhile the Democratic Liberal Party was eager to hold an early election to take advantage of the failures of the Socialist and Democratic Party coalition government which collapsed in the autumn of 1948 as a result of a separate bribery scandal involving another priority production industry – fertilisers – called the Showa Denko scandal. Therefore, Democratic Liberal moves for a snap election were made over the objection of the other parties, theoretically in the majority, and even the key elements in the US-dominated Allied occupation. A compromise was reached whereby the Socialist and Democratic coalition government budget was passed with Democratic Liberal Party support and the Democratic Liberals were permitted to hold their election.

The Democratic Liberal Party tried to distance itself from Tanaka by pointing out that he was a Democratic Party MP when the alleged incident was supposed to have occurred. Yet at the same time, Tanaka was allowed to run as a Democratic Liberal Party candidate in the January 1949 election when he was forced to fight for his seat from jail. It was a tough battle for Tanaka but he won re-election and joined in the landslide victory for the Democratic Liberal Party which savaged their Socialist and Democratic opponents, whose number of MPs fell by more than half. Ominously, the Communist Party seemed to have gained at the expense of the Socialists, but the Democratic Liberals had a solid majority and were set to govern the country for the next parliament which lasted until 1952. Tanaka was convicted of bribery in 1950, but he was found innocent on appeal in 1951 just in time for the next election.

The main lesson that Tanaka learned from the entire incident is that he could get away with bribery. There is little doubt that he accepted a bribe, since the man who gave him the money openly admitted his involvement many years later.[20] More significantly, a number of politicians associated with Tanaka who complained about being involved in his shady transactions are reported to have heard him brag that a man is not a man until he has been imprisoned once or twice. This logic was not unlike that of the *yakuza* dons whom Tanaka associated with and seemed to emulate over the years. Unsurprisingly, Tanaka was behind many of the major political corruption scandals of postwar Japan.

Postwar corruption involving organised crime and extreme nationalists stands in sharp contrast to pre-war corruption in Japan. Pre-war corruption involved the elite and was severely criticised by the military and nationalistic right. As we have seen, the wartime regime and immediate postwar situation created corruption which was more democratic by providing wider opportunities for advancement, so the populist appeal of attacks on the corrupt, wealthy elite lost their salience. After the war, the military were gone and nationalist groups were deeply involved in the corrupt underground of Japanese politics.[21] Moreover, the war, postwar inflation, *zaibatsu* dissolution, land reform, and many of the other changes to Japan effectively levelled Japanese society and destroyed the pre-war order. Tanaka and his dubious associates were models, even heroes, of a new generation of Japanese who still struggled to make a place for themselves in the new Japan.

. . .

THE CREATION OF A 'NEW' ELITE

Tanaka's political activities also signal one of the most significant changes in Japanese politics after the war: the transformation of party organisation at the local level. Unlike pre-war party notables such as landlords and local merchants, the Liberal Party began to build its party organisation on a new type of local notable, such as the local elected officials who would also often serve as the heads of a local administrative body, such as an agricultural co-operative.

The war had already begun the process of creating a new class of bureaucratic and elected officials with the competence and authority to supplant 'traditional' notables. Postwar reforms merely accentuated the process.[22] This was especially true of the land reform committees. Despite complaints about the officious and obstructionist attitudes of local functionaries, people were often grateful for the assistance of a particular individual in working through the complex process of land reform or other postwar institutional reforms.[23]

The success of the Liberals in attracting support from small business has been emphasised, and this was true in both rural areas, such as among coal mine operators, and urban areas, among merchants. For example, in Tokyo,[24] merchant support of the Liberal Party was reinforced by antagonism to Socialist government restrictions on commerce. This support for the Liberals extended to the merchants organised into retail co-operatives (*shogyo kumiai*). Moreover, many manufacturers, primarily suppliers for larger firms, who had often supported the Democratic Party or the Socialists, switched to the Liberal Party by 1949.

New notables emerged who were often elected local officials in local government, farm co-operatives and even farmers and labour unions. These leaders in turn organised their membership more on the basis of shared interests than individual benefits. In this way, the conservatives too were forced to build a mass organisational strategy, and one that in the end resulted in weakening the impersonal mass mobilisation strategies of the left through the substitution of a more personal leadership focused mass strategy. This process constitutes the origin of the postwar Japanese electoral support organisation of the conservatives, the *koenkai* (see pp. 41–5 for details of these).[25]

This new elite included gangster-like bosses and dubious entrepreneurs such as Tanaka, who crudely spread their money far and wide. To a degree, gift-giving customs and payments to smooth negotiations which were not uncommon in pre-war Japan became more widespread as more could afford to imitate the old elite. Tanaka's approach to the use of money in politics was therefore not entirely unique in the context of immediate postwar Japan. He was part of a new self-made elite which, despite their dubious origins and political methods, constituted the foundation for postwar politics. As we shall see in the next chapters, economic growth in Japan reinforced and was reinforced by a style of money politics which did not originate with Tanaka, but which he came to represent by the scale on which he practised it and the way in which his behaviour compelled others to imitate him.

. . .

NOTES AND REFERENCES

1 Takashi Tachibana, *Tanaka Kakuei Kenkyu Zenkiryoku* [A Study of Kakuei Tanaka: The Full Record], vol. 1 (1982), p. 64.

2 John Dower, *Japan in War and Peace* (London, 1993), pp. 13–14.

3 Masumi Junnosuke, *Nihon Seito Shi Ron* [On the History of Japanese Political Parties], vol. 7 (1984).

4 Gordon Wright, *The Ordeal of Total War, 1939–1945* (New York, 1968), p. 246.

5 Harry Emerson Wildes, 'Postwar Politics in Japan II: IV. Underground Politics in Postwar Japan', *American Political Science Review*, vol. 42, no. 6 (December 1948), p. 1152.

6 *Ibid.*, p. 1156.

7 Masumi Ishikawa, *Jinbutsu Sengo Seiji* [People in Postwar Politics] (1997), pp. 84–5.

8 Kenzo Uchida, 'Japan's Postwar Conservative Parties', in Robert Ward and Yoshikazu Sakamoto (eds), *Democratizing Japan: The Allied Occupation* (Honolulu, HI, 1987), p. 315.

9 Wildes, 'Underground Politics in Postwar Japan', p. 1153.

10 Masumi Junnosuke, *Politics in Postwar Japan, 1945–1955* (Berkeley, CA, 1985), p. 84.

11 Kakuei Tanaka, *Watakushi no Rirekisho* [My Curriculum Vitae] (1966), pp. 165–6.

12 Labour statistics for the period are lacking but indirect evidence, such as the peak level of wartime production, indicates that the industrial workforce must have grown dramatically unless productivity had increased dramatically then disappeared after the war, which is unlikely. See the charts in Kimihiro Masamura, *Zusetsu Sengo Shi* [A Postwar History in Charts] (1988), p. 47.

13 Sasada Shigeru, *Nihon Shakaito* [Japan Socialist Party], vol. 1 (1960), p. 94.

14 Shigeyoshi Kiso, 'Saigo no Chusho Tanko' [The Last Small- and Medium-sized Coal Mine] in Kanichi Kondo and Hiroshi Osanai (eds), *Sengo Sangyo Shi e no Shogen* [Testimonies on Postwar Industrial History] (1978), pp. 110–22.

15 Richard Samuels, *The Business of the Japanese State* (Ithaca, NY, 1987), p. 98.

16 *Ibid.*

17 Saki Ryuzo, *Tanaka Kakuei no Fukei: Sengo Shoki Tanko Giwaku* [The Background of Tanaka Kakuei: The Early Postwar Coal Control Scandal] (1983).

18 Shigeyoshi, 'Saigo no Chusho Tanko', p. 113.

19 Tachibana, *Tanaka Kakuei Kenkyu*, p. 68.

20 Shigeyoshi, 'Saigo no Chusho Tanko', p. 113.

21 There have been exceptions, as some isolated individuals and groups still attack the conservative leadership for corruption, but more likely than not right-wing groups have close ties and affinities with the most corrupt conservative politicians.

22 Masumi, *Politics in Postwar Japan, 1945–1955*, p. 231.

23 *Sengo Taiken* [The Postwar Experience] (1981), p. 32.

24 Masamichi Royama, *Sosenkyo no Jittai* [The Reality of General Elections] (1955), pp. 73–4.

25 Gerald Curtis, *Election Campaigning Japanese Style* (1971), pp. 126–30, 251–2. Curtis notes that *koenkai* are a postwar phenomenon which substituted local officials and voluntary associations for the landlords and notables of pre-war Japan, but neither Curtis, nor the literature he cites, discuss the process by which this transformation was made in any detail.

Chapter 3

TANAKA-STYLE POPULISM

By the time of his opposition to coal nationalisation, if not earlier, Tanaka had developed a distinct distaste for socialism. It was his opposition to coal nationalisation which led Tanaka to quit the Democratic Party and join the Liberal Party in early 1948. The coalition was also having trouble coping with hyperinflation and a sluggish economic recovery blamed by many on its interventionist policies. The need for postwar austerity measures, especially a massive reduction in the number of government employees and subsidies to industry, was increasingly apparent by 1948. As a result of this experience, Tanaka would never adopt an approach to policy-making that was based on nationalisation of industry or direct governmental control of economic life.

Instead, the type of legislation that Tanaka proposed as a junior MP focused on building the infrastructure which was to prove essential to Japan's postwar economic miracle. In identifying the need for such spending, Tanaka cultivated relationships with bureaucrats who were certainly interventionist and in some cases clearly socialist in their orientation. Moreover, Tanaka's ability to achieve re-election with increasing levels of voter support in his district was the result of his wooing of rural voters, including former socialist voters, with concrete benefits drawn from his government connections.

This approach has been called Tanaka-style socialism, but it is better viewed as a form of right-wing populism. The same type of populist approach was adopted by the Prime Minister of Japan at the end of the 1950s, Nobusuke Kishi, who gave Tanaka his first cabinet post in 1957. In short, the 1950s was the period in which the foundations of Japanese economic success were created through a combination of public works, patronage and populism.

. . .

JOINING THE YOSHIDA SCHOOL

At the beginning of the 1950s, Tanaka was savvy enough to make the shift early to the opposite end of the conservative political spectrum from the conservatives who dominated the wartime regime and the Democratic Party. He not only transferred his allegiance to the opposition Liberal Party but became an important supporter of Shigeru Yoshida, the Prime Minister who dominated Japan's first postwar decade.

Siding with Yoshida was not an obvious choice given Tanaka's background. Yoshida was a former Foreign Ministry official and a member of Japan's pre-war elite. He was also critical and suspicious of the very same groups and individuals with whom Tanaka had been associated during and immediately after the war. Yoshida's conversion to market liberalism and a distaste for the militaristic right were not completely shared by Tanaka. Worse, Yoshida was out of power and even though the Socialist–Democratic Party coalition seemed likely to collapse, key members of the US Occupation authorities were so opposed to Yoshida that there was no guarantee that he would continue to be a powerful ally who might help Tanaka.

The route taken by Tanaka in aligning himself with Yoshida, who dominated Japanese politics for most of the first postwar decade, is difficult to determine precisely. He and 17 other MPs quit the Democratic Party three days after the passage of the Coal Control Act and formed the Democratic Club. In March 1948, immediately after the formation of Hitoshi Ashida's cabinet – another coalition government involving the Democratic Party and the Socialists – the Democratic Club and the Daiichi Giin Club, a parliamentary group composed of unaffiliated politicians, joined with the Liberal Party to form the Democratic Liberal Party.[1] This move by Tanaka and others was significant as the first sign of the revival in the Liberals' fortunes but there is no evidence that Tanaka was prominent at this point.

This strengthening of Yoshida's party was followed by the formation of the so-called 'Yoshida school': on 21 July 1948, Yoshida brought together a number of top-level bureaucrats and invited them to join the Liberals, and on the following day, he announced to the press that 28 such officials were joining his party to run for national office in the next general election.[2] Most were officials at the level of administrative vice-minister or section chief class and

37

their defection was a major blow to the coalition government. Tanaka was able to become a 'pupil' in the Yoshida school and was one of only a few politicians among a group predominantly bureaucratic in origin. Tanaka became particularly close to one of the key members of the Yoshida school, the former Transport Ministry bureaucrat Eisaku Sato, and he was the probable source of Tanaka's access to Yoshida's inner circle. As a result of defections and serious divisions between and within the parties of the coalition, the Ashida government collapsed at the end of the summer of 1948, and the Liberal Party under Yoshida was given responsibility for forming a caretaker government in October 1948. There was one problem, however: the Government Section of the General Headquarters of Supreme Commander of the Allies in the Pacific (SCAP), the key agency of the US-led Occupation, was actively involved in trying to block Yoshida's return to power. In the latter half of September 1948, Liberal Party representative Yukuichiro Yamaguchi was summoned by Justin Williams, the Government Section bureau chief responsible for parliamentary matters, who suggested that it was necessary to 'deal with' Yoshida if the Liberal Party wanted to form a cabinet.[3] Yamaguchi joined with Jiro Hoshijima to work to replace Yoshida with Liberal Party director Takeshi Yamazaki. At one point, the scheme appeared to have broad support extending all the way to the Socialists. Yamazaki, however, was not up to the task, and not only backed down on the challenge to Yoshida, but was persuaded to resign his seat in parliament. Tanaka later claimed that it was he who persuaded Yamazaki to back down and permitted Yoshida to regain power.

If true, the event goes some way to indicate how Tanaka, a relatively unknown junior MP, began to play such a prominent role in Japanese politics in the years following. Yoshida's victory over the Occupation was a seminal event. It demonstrated the limits of the Occupation to alter the course of Japanese domestic political events. While Charles Kades, assistant section chief at Government Section and Williams's direct superior, for one, has attempted to deny that the Occupation opposed the Liberals – he claims that they were only opposed to Yoshida personally – he cannot deny that the Occupation had failed to remove a politician openly hostile to them.[4] Once safely back in power, Yoshida immediately attempted to move to dissolve the parliament and force a new election which the Liberals easily won. This set the stage for the implementation of a strict austerity programme, known as the Dodge line after the US businessman Joseph Merrill Dodge, sent by the US to advise the Japanese government on reducing public spending. As a result of the slashing of subsidies to industry and lay-offs of large numbers of government employees, particularly in public corporations such as Japan's National Railways, an economic recession ensued. Tanaka's own business was directly affected by the downturn. He reorganised Tanaka Construction by reducing his capital from 5 million to 1 million yen and the number of his employees from over 200 to less than 50 as he concentrated his efforts on the Tokyo region by shutting down branches across the country.[5] At the same time, he began to rely heavily on his family relations as members of the board not only of Tanaka Construction but also of a number of related real estate and development companies as he poised himself for an improvement in the national economic situation which was not long in coming.

. . .

ECONOMIC GROWTH, PLANNING AND PATRONAGE

The outbreak of the Korean War in June 1950 gave the first boost to the postwar Japanese economy, and though the miracle economy is usually associated with the 1960s, the foundations for high levels of economic growth were established in the 1950s. These foundations might be strongly associated with the bureaucracy in Japan, but there was a political dimension to the institutions of growth, and in this context, Tanaka played a key role in creating the institutional infrastructure of postwar economic recovery. At the same time, Tanaka gained politically from the benefits which he began to channel to his constituents and personally as a result of shrewd corporate and land deals through his burgeoning network of companies.

The Korean War boom was a crucial starting point for the postwar Japanese economy because it led to large orders of industrial goods by United Nations forces, mainly the United States, and this enabled Japan in 1951 to exceed the pre-war volume of industrial production for the first time since 1944.[6] Without foreign military procurement Japan would not have earned the income necessary to re-equip her industry and restore pre-war levels of consumption. Even after the end of the war boom, Japan's economy continued to grow despite occasional short recessions induced by monetary authorities to control inflation. By 1955:

> economic expansion was resumed at a faster rate than ever and by 1957 it could be said that Japanese recovery was complete. Most of her industries had been re-equipped and reorganised. Industrial production was probably over two and a half times the pre-war volume, gross national product in real terms about 50 per cent higher and national income perhaps 10 per cent higher.[7]

Chalmers Johnson has examined the institutions of high-speed growth in this period, particularly the role of the powerful Ministry of International Trade and Industry which had near complete control over foreign trade and the introduction of foreign technology. Using the remnants of wartime and Occupation era controls, the ministry 'single-mindedly turned the Japanese industrial structure from light, labor-intensive industries to steel, ships and automobiles of which Japan is the leading producer today'.[8] Thus, one key factor in any explanation of Japan's remarkable growth is infrastructure. Without adequate power supplies, factories could not operate. Without roads and port facilities, goods could not be transported and exported. Even if one focuses on private sector dynamism as the key to Japan's postwar growth, one cannot ignore the bureaucratic and politically driven development of industrial infrastructure in the 1950s which made such private activity possible.

Though still a comparatively young politician in the period, Tanaka played a leading role in key legislation to provide the infrastructure to rebuild Japan. Much of this legislation was put forward as private members' bills, and so many pieces of legislation for industrial development were passed as a result of his efforts that he was even dubbed 'Mr. Private Member's Bill'. Perhaps the most outstanding example of Tanaka's efforts was the legislation associated with road building. When Tanaka was growing up in Niigata, paved roads were rare and he no doubt had first-hand experience of the problems of inadequate roads in a region snowbound in the winter and a quagmire in the spring. In 1953, he helped to pass a law imposing a tax on gasoline in order to fund the building of new roads. The tax – still in effect – funded the expansion of Japan's road network dramatically after the war.

In promoting this legislation, as in much of his political activities, Tanaka had to manage against formidable opposition. The Ministry of Finance, for example, opposed the gasoline tax because it was opposed to hypothecation – i.e. any special allocation of tax receipts, which it felt should all go to the general budget – and the transport and oil industries were also opposed to the new tax.[9] However, Tanaka persevered – almost single-handedly – and persuaded his fellow MPs of the importance of the legislation. He also made some creative compromises. He agreed that a special account need not be created for the tax receipts so long as the general account always disbursed more in road construction funds than it took in gasoline taxes.[10] This project had the support of Eisaku Sato, Minister of Construction at the time and a key member of the Yoshida government, and so was passed in July 1953.

Tanaka was also able to persuade the Construction Ministry of the need for a long-term plan for the building of motorways in Japan. At first the ministry opposed the plan, arguing that there were no resources to fund the construction of an extensive high-speed road network, and even when Tanaka suggested that the introduction of a toll road system would solve the problem, Construction Ministry bureaucrats – who believed that government-built roads should be free of charge – were sceptical of the plan until Tanaka was able to show them that in fact a minor toll road did exist. The bureaucrats could not argue against precedent.[11] With his persistence, creative planning and a good sense of psychology, Tanaka became highly skilled at managing powerful and conflicting forces in the government, and effectively, the postwar road network in Japan – the heart of the postwar Japanese economy – was conceived and implemented by Tanaka.

. . .

KOENKAI AND THE BUILDING OF CONSERVATIVE SUPPORT

Public works projects, such as roads, were also a source of patronage, and Tanaka used his patronage to build one of the strongest constituency groups in Japan – a model for conservatives throughout the country. Indeed, Tanaka's political style was the most effective in combating the rise of the Socialists, especially in areas such as Niigata which had been a natural political target for the Socialists. As the Socialists appeared to be recovering their strength, so Tanaka's skills in wooing voters would not be ignored.

As we have seen, Tanaka did not have the strongest support base in Niigata at the beginning of his political career, but by the end of the decade he had one of the most secure seats in the prefecture. The main reason for this success was the provision of concrete benefits to the voters in his district. In addition to the general legislative initiatives to build roads and improve infrastructure, Tanaka made sure that the implementation of government plans favoured his supporters.

For example, when the state-owned Electric Power Development Corporation was created in 1952 to develop Japan's electricity supply by acquiring land and building dams to provide hydroelectric power – passed as a private member's bill – Tanaka influenced the siting of the Tadamigawa Dam to the benefit of Niigata prefecture, which was embroiled in a water rights dispute with neighbouring Fukushima prefecture, and to the benefit of landowners of the dam site, not to mention construction firms and local residents who would work at the facility. It was alleged that he received pay-offs for his actions, but no charges were brought.[12]

Tanaka operated on a more private level as well. For example, when the small Nagaoka Railroad Company appeared to be about to go under in 1950 because it could not find the capital it needed to electrify the service, Tanaka was approached. Company officials believed Tanaka had the clout to mobilise the resources needed to save the line from closure. At first, Tanaka refused, arguing that it was not his area of the district and they should approach their local MP instead. However, the local MP had refused because the task was enormously difficult even if the service it provided was essential to the local people in the area. After being approached several times, Tanaka relented but agreed to help only if he had the complete co-operation of the stockholders, union officials and the users of the service. The stockholders voted overwhelmingly to elect Tanaka president of Nagaoka. One year later, Tanaka not only managed to use his business connections to secure funding from the Japan Development Bank and other financial institutions, he also had the work completed on schedule. When a snap election was held in 1952, Tanaka gained the most votes of any candidate in the district, helped by the votes from that part of the district served by the Nagaoka Railroad where his vote increased by nearly four times compared to the previous election. The local MP who had refused to help fell to last place among those elected from the district.[13]

Tanaka's ability to bring concrete benefits to his constituency attracted support from across the political spectrum. As Satomi Tani notes:

> [Tanaka] obtained many public works projects for his constituency in Niigata Prefecture and secured overwhelming voter support. In contrast, Shoichi Miyake, a former leader of the tenant movement in Niigata and later vice-speaker of the lower house, proved either ineffective or reluctant to engage in pork barrel politics. Whenever his constituents asked him to influence the central bureaucracy to do something for their villages and towns, they were disappointed; many voters who once supported the JSP switched to Tanaka and the LDP and became part of Tanaka's political machine.[14]

Activists as well as voters switched from the Socialist Party to support Tanaka. While Tanaka hated communism and socialism, the positions he espoused about the need for equality of opportunity and assistance for the needy were not inconsistent with the views of many on the left who drifted into his camp from the Socialists in the early 1950s.[15] This situation was not unique to Tanaka's district. As urbanisation progressed and the opposition parties grew stronger as a result, the Liberal Democratic Party (see pp. 62–3) set out to increase its hold on rural districts and succeeded in reducing the once strong Socialist presence in rural Japan to a shadow of its former level within ten years of land reform.

It is also significant that the conservatives encouraged wider participation in their party. Like most conservative MPs then and now, Tanaka organised his local supporters into a *koenkai*, a postwar phenomenon which incorporated the new elites in a more inclusive electoral organisation than the handful of notables of the pre-war political parties. To a large degree, this was the conservative response to the branch structure of the Socialists, but they still retained a more exclusive image with the leading members of local society playing a prominent role. Yet, unlike party branches, *koenkai* have varied greatly in character. Some have been relatively small, composed mainly of local MPs, officials in local governmental organisations, the local agricultural co-operatives, business leaders and chairmen of chambers of commerce as well as priests of local temples and shrines. Others have been massive groups involving average voters in informational and entertainment activities. Most have been somewhere in between.[16]

The Etsuzankai was a particularly large and inclusive organisation, and compared to other *koenkai* it was more deeply involved in the lives of constituents. It would act as a conciliator in disputes between husband and wife, give business advice, help solve problems between young wives and mothers-in-law, and help students to get into the schools they wanted and others to get jobs. An association of those helped to gain employment by the Etsuzankai was formed with as many as 3,000 members who met annually in Tokyo to give a party for Tanaka. At election time, the Etsuzankai volunteers would call on those helped in this way to go to the polls and vote for Tanaka. Different branches of the organisation would compete to see who could achieve the highest vote totals.[17]

Given the extensiveness of the tasks required, it is no surprise that the Etsuzankai had branches throughout the district, many of which were staffed by former war buddies and others with deep ties to Tanaka. One top official in the Etsuzankai was Akiko Sato, a woman whom Tanaka helped through a divorce and took into his protection. She soon became his secretary and mistress, and in August 1958 she bore him a daughter. Though he never legally recognised this illegitimate daughter, he always brought her presents and spent time with her when he could, and Akiko Sato understood that a rising politician could not do more without damaging his career.[18] For Tanaka, the distinction between generosity, personal desires and political needs was often blurred.

The Etsuzankai was also an effective means of gathering funds and mobilising support, but it would be a mistake to assume that this was an organisation centred on corruption. There is no evidence that Tanaka crudely bought votes for cash. If anything, the Etsuzankai was a source of funds rather than a conduit to bribe supporters. Like any good Japanese politician at the time, Tanaka was generous in his gifts to married couples and bereaved families in his district. In addition, he did not forget his supporters at election time. At the same time, the benefits he brought to his district were diffuse. Particular projects and even jobs might be credited to him, but he also benefited from the general economic recovery, particularly in the late 1950s.

The new consumer boom of the late 1950s was itself a product of the new postwar democracy. In pre-war Japan, the residents of areas such as Niigata were seen as a source of labour for export industries rather than as part of an essential market for Japanese goods. Economic policy before the war focused on keeping wages low and sending the best goods overseas to earn valuable foreign exchange. After the war, foreign exchange was still scarce in Japan, and access to it was restricted to the essential manufacturing industries that formed the basis of Japan's postwar miracle, but this also meant that the rich could not import luxury goods such as foreign cars. Instead, all Japanese were encouraged to aspire to purchase domestic-made consumer goods. It was in this period when the three treasures of the Imperial family (an ancient mirror, sword and sceptre) were turned into a slogan for the three consumer goods all Japanese could naturally aspire to acquire: a refrigerator, a washing machine and a television.

. . .

THE EMERGENCE OF FACTION POLITICS

The booming economy did not help Yoshida and the Liberals, however, who were finally brought down after six years of continuous control of government in the general election of 1955. In some sense, Yoshida had been in decline since the end of the Allied occupation in 1952 when his abrasive, confrontational style suddenly began to seem less necessary, but other issues also played a role. The key issue raised before the election was a scandal involving the shipbuilding industry which reached up into the highest levels of the Yoshida government, implicating in particular Eisaku Sato, Tanaka's mentor. When the Liberal Party Minister of Justice used his powers to block any prosecution of Sato as a result of the affair, public opinion turned strongly against the Liberal Party. The Liberals had been in power too long and were growing as corrupt as their predecessors.

The Liberals' conservative opponents, the Democratic Party, won the most seats in the 1955 election and formed a government, though they still lacked a majority in parliament. Business leaders, fearing another coalition with the Socialists who had gained electorally in recent years and had unified into a more cohesive political force, persuaded the Liberal and Democratic Parties to merge in late 1955. Tanaka was now one of a number of influential MPs in a much larger conservative party.

One problem with the new party, the Liberal Democratic Party (LDP), was that there was no certainty that it would last, nor could the possibility of continuing Socialist gains be ignored. Today, after over 40 years of LDP dominance of Japanese government, it is difficult to realise that the success of the merger of the Liberal and Democratic Parties was not a foregone conclusion. Certainly, there was strong opposition to the move in both parties.[19] Distaste was particularly strong among the 13 key members of the Yoshida group in the Liberal Party, including Tanaka, and reformist conservatives, including Takeo Miki, who feared the new party would be dominated by their right-wing conservative opponents. In the end, however, the Yoshida group and the Miki forces were too small to survive outside the party and felt compelled to go along.

Fortunately for Tanaka, however, neither of the Prime Ministers who succeeded Yoshida, Hatoyama and Ishibashi, lasted long as both were old men tired by years of political struggle. Upon the early retirement of Ishibashi due to ill health, Nobusuke Kishi became Prime Minister in February 1957. In general, those opposed to the Kishi administration were the same as those who had been against the merger of the Liberal and Democratic Parties in 1955, including the former Yoshida group now led by Ikeda and the old Democratic Party progressives led by Takeo Miki.

One group of former Yoshida supporters, however, did play a role in the creation of the Kishi government: the faction emerging around Eisaku Sato. Sato was Kishi's brother, though he had been raised by different parents; more importantly, he shared Kishi's right-wing political views despite having been associated with Yoshida while Yoshida was in power. As Tanaka was a leading member of the Sato faction, he was given the position of Minister of Posts and Telecommunication in the Kishi cabinet of July 1957. It is also widely rumoured that Tanaka passed Kishi 3,000,000 yen stuffed into a backpack as a payment for the post. Whatever the reason, Tanaka was the youngest MP ever to have been selected as a cabinet minister.

As Posts and Telecommunication Minister, Tanaka was responsible for the granting of licences for local television stations throughout Japan over the objections of the bureaucrats in his own ministry who felt that the industry was not ready for expansion.[20] He recognised the importance of television before most other politicians, not just in Japan but in the rest of the world as well. He appeared on popular television programmes, even singing Japanese folk ballads (*naniwa bushi*) in his rough voice. He was such a success that he released a vinyl record which sold well and was frequently heard on radio throughout Japan. Tanaka was suddenly a nationally known figure.

He also became a protector of the Japanese postal savings system which maintained more branches and held more assets than any financial institution in Japan. The postal savings system was politically important as a source of cheap capital which the government provided to favoured industries, as a tax-free haven for savings and as a connection to post office branch managers who played a key role in *koenkai* across Japan. Tanaka also fought to reduce the influence of the powerful Telecommunication Workers Union, which supported the Socialist Party, by firing a tenth of their workforce, or 22,000 workers.[21] From this point forward, Tanaka was the main political patron and contact point for the postal and telecommunication industry and bureaucracy.

Tanaka also learned much about politics from Kishi. When the ambitions of faction leader Ichiro Kono began to appear as a threat to Kishi, Kishi deftly substituted the former Yoshida group leader Ikeda into the coalition in support of his government while denying Kono the benefits of office. This not only marginalised Kono but weakened internal opposition by co-opting Ikeda. Thus, the role of ideological proximity weakened and personal ties to a leading politician became more important. While it is true that junior politicians had often made alliances with senior party leaders and these relationships had been cemented by the provision of political funds to create competing groups around individuals as far back as the pre-war period, with the creation of the LDP more emphasis was placed on personal ties and less on ideological differences. The result was the creation of the typical postwar faction with a non-ideological, personal style of politics very congenial to Tanaka and his way of doing things.

However, Kishi's government fell after only a little over three years. The main reason for the demise of Kishi was widespread opposition to his forcing through a Revised Security Treaty with the United States in what is often viewed as the classic confrontation between the postwar Japanese left and right. The treaty gave the US military facilities throughout Japan, permitted the US to use these bases to engage in military actions without the Japanese government's approval, and allowed the US to intervene unilaterally in Japan militarily if US security interests were threatened. Opposition to the treaty on the left was fierce, because it appeared to be directed at the communist states of Asia, with which the left had strong sympathies, and because it had the potential to involve Japan in US military conflicts against the pacifist inclinations of the left and the majority of the Japanese people. The anti-Security Treaty movement invigorated the Japanese left, giving it an issue with which to appeal to Japanese nationalism.

Kishi's use of right-wing groups and gangsters to intimidate protesters also raised the spectre of right-wing politicians' use of extra-parliamentary fringe elements in Japanese society to achieve their goals. These underground elements permeated the highest levels of Japanese society and Tanaka was as disposed as Kishi to rely on them when needed. These tactics did much to undermine Kishi, and the use of such forces by Tanaka and his successors would also eventually contribute to their downfall.

Kishi himself, however, believed that he was undercut on issues such as treaty renewal and constitutional revision as much by those in his own party, especially anti-mainstream former progressives such as Takeo Miki, as by those on the left who took to the streets. Even Ikeda, who had shifted to support of the Kishi administration, positioned himself in such a way as to take advantage of Kishi's demise by portraying himself as the acceptable face of mainstream conservatism. While Kishi's resignation and the beginning of the Ikeda administration constituted a new phase in Japanese politics, the danger of betrayal by other faction leaders was a problem faced by all subsequent Japanese prime ministers and also contributed to Tanaka's downfall.

. . .

CONCLUSION

The 1950s saw the emergence of the Liberal Democratic Party and the three pillars of LDP success: high levels of economic growth, pay-offs to core constituencies and the management of internal conservative conflict through factionalism. Tanaka was at the centre of each of these developments in Japanese politics, and in the years that followed he pushed these trends even further. We have seen that Tanaka played a key role in creating the foundations for further economic growth. His political innovations at the local level were also notable. While Tanaka's *koenkai* support organisation was not unique, it was extremely successful and would be even more so as time passed, giving rise to a legend that no politician could ignore. Moreover, Tanaka's local strategy of patronage eventually became public policy at the national level. Finally, Tanaka learned much from Kishi's success in factional politics and the cost of betrayal. For the immediate future, however, Tanaka's ties to Ikeda and Sato, as a member of the old Yoshida group, smoothed the path for his continuing survival. Indeed, since Ikeda and Sato dominated Japanese politics in the 1960s, Tanaka was well positioned to succeed.

. . .

NOTES AND REFERENCES

1 For the sake of clarity, I will continue to refer to this party as the Liberal Party hereafter.

2 Motoma Kansan, 'Kanryo To Shinjin Ron' [On the New Bureaucratic Party Members], *Saiken*, vol. 3, no. 1 (Jan. 1949), pp. 2–3.

3 Eiji Tominomori, *Sengo Hoshuto Shi* [Postwar Conservative Party History] (1994), pp. 26–7.

4 Eiji Takamae, 'Kedisu Nihon Senryo Kaishiroku' [Kades Memoir on the Occupation of Japan], *Tokyo Seizai Daigaku Kaishi*, no. 148 (Nov. 1986), pp. 305–6. [In English with a Japanese summary.]

5 Takashi Tachibana, *Tanaka Kakuei Kenkyu Senkiryoku* [A Study of Kakuei Tanaka: The Full Record], vol. 1 (1982), pp. 70–1.

6 G.C. Allen, *A Short Economic History of Modern Japan* (New York, 1963), p. 172.

7 *Ibid.*, pp. 173–4.

8 Chalmers Johnson, *MITI and the Japanese Miracle* (Stanford, CA, 1982), p. 240.

9 Yoh Mizuki, *Tanaka Kakuei: Sono Kyozen to Kyoaku* [Kakuei Tanaka: His Greatness and Wickedness] (1998), p. 83.

10 *Ibid.*, p. 84.

11 *Ibid.*, p. 85.

12 Richard Samuels, *The Business of the Japanese State* (Ithaca, NY, 1987), p. 161.

13 Mizuki, *Tanaka Kakuei*, pp. 60–3.

14 Satomi Tani, 'The Japan Socialist Party before the Mid-1960s: An Analysis of Its Stagnation', in Tetsuya Kataoka (ed.), *Creating Single Party Democracy: Japan's Postwar Political System* (Stanford, CA, 1992), p. 94. For a definition of the term 'pork barrel politics', see Chapter 1, p. 9.

15 Mizuki, *Tanaka Kakuei*, pp. 68–71; Toru Hayano, *Tanaka Kakuei to 'Sengo' no Seishin* [Kakuei Tanaka and the 'Spirit' of Postwar Japan] (1995), pp. 56–8.

16 Gerald Curtis, *Election Campaigning Japan Style* (1971), pp. 126–33.

17 Kichiya Kobayashi, *Jitsuryoku Etsuzankai* [The Etsuzan Association: A True Record] (1979), pp. 109–11.
18 Akiko Sato, *Watashi no Tanaka Kakuei Nikki* [My Kakuei Tanaka Diary] (1994), p. 45.
19 Isamu Tagawa, *Tanaka Kakuei to Seiken no Toso* [Kakuei Tanaka and the Struggle for Political Power] (1982), p. 121.
20 Mizuki, *Tanaka Kakuei*, pp. 88–90.
21 *Ibid.*, p. 89.

Chapter 4

MIRACLE WORKER

The 1960s was the era of the Japanese economic miracle. While Japan's economy recovery had begun in the 1950s, the period of highest postwar economic growth was in the decade that followed. It is true that all major industrialised economies experienced high growth during the years 1960 to 1969, and 3.1 per cent growth in the United Kingdom and 4.1 per cent in the United States helped to create the swinging sixties. Economic recovery in West Germany at 5.7 per cent during the same period was also hailed as an economic miracle, but Japanese economic growth averaged 12.1 per cent even after adjustment for inflation.[1] Japan's hosting of the 1964 Olympics in Tokyo and the high-speed bullet trains (*shinkansen*), which connected a modern Tokyo to the ancient capital and tourist destination Kyoto, symbolised the new economic prowess of Japan.

At the time, most Japanese and many Western observers believed it was Japanese hard work and long hours that made the economic miracle possible. Subsequent economic analysis has suggested that capital investment, new technology and the transfer of labour between farming and manufacturing also played a major role in creating the basis for economic growth.[2] One of the most outstanding features of Japanese growth, however, was the expansion of markets which provided economies of scale.[3]

In sharp contrast to the low wage strategy of pre-war industrialists and economic policy-makers, democratisation in postwar Japan meant that the demands of farmers and organised labour could not be ignored. Farmers were given subsidies to support their livelihoods, though not so much that they could afford to ignore work opportunities in urban areas where many of them moved permanently. Organised labour was recognised by law, and despite divisive

51

strikes in the 1950s, a compromise was reached by the end of that decade whereby unions would avoid strikes in exchange for job security and regular wage increases. This was the beginning of the Japanese system of lifetime employment and the seniority-based wage scale. In essence, the rise of the common people through increased democracy and the creation of a mass consumer market made the economic miracle possible.

The government which followed Kishi at the beginning of the 1960s, that of Hayato Ikeda, built on these foundations by a policy of avoiding confrontation with labour and the left. The emphasis switched from politics to economics as Ikeda announced a plan to double Japanese per capita income by the end of the decade. Companies were encouraged to transfer the benefits of growth to their employees and in turn they spent their higher incomes on the purchase of consumer goods which gave a further boost to economic growth. As in the late 1950s, so the 1960s was also the period of three new Imperial treasures – car, cooler and colour television – with dramatic consequences for the key automobile, steel, rubber, consumer electronics and other related manufacturing industries. This created a virtuous circle of growth based on domestic demand as profits went into wages and wages increased consumer demand which caused profits to grow.

This picture of domestic demand-led growth often surprises those who believe that Japan relied on exports to grow, but such a belief is a legacy of the low-cost export strategy of pre-war undemocratic Japan and of Japan's occasional attempts to export itself out of recession. Nonetheless, exports *were* important to Japan which has few natural resources of its own so has to import (and pay for) most of its energy supplies, raw materials and key foodstuffs.

Japan benefited in its period of high growth from a stable international system under the United States' political and economic hegemony. The US promoted free market access to inexpensive raw materials, and worked to keep prices low on key commodities such as crude oil. Japan also took full advantage of the latest American technologies, to which access was open in a way that seems almost naive today. Finally, not only did Japan have open access to the large and affluent US market but the US also tolerated the protectionism of the Japanese market. Japan sold televisions and cars in the United States but almost no comparable US goods were sold in Japan at the time due to formal and informal import restrictions. Thus, the gains of domestic growth in Japan went to Japanese firms and were not repatriated abroad. The favourable exchange rate of 360 yen to the dollar under the US-backed Bretton Woods system of fixed exchange rates ensured that Japanese goods were competitive in the US market but that foreign goods were too expensive for most Japanese to even contemplate buying even if they were available.

. . .

BUREAUCRATS IN THE ECONOMY AND POLITICS

There is also a third explanation for Japanese economic growth – in addition to the favourable conditions created by the United States and the domestic demand created by postwar democratic reforms – and that is the crucial role played by the Japanese bureaucracy in coordinating the allocation of resources and Japan's interaction with the outside world. The most important power of the bureaucracy was held by the Ministry of International Trade and Industry (MITI), which effectively held the power of veto over the allocation of scarce foreign exchange. In an economy such as Japan's, for which the importation of raw materials and technology was (and is) crucial, the power to deny access to foreign exchange was all-important.

MITI used its power to direct resources to manufacturing and export industries, and to deny firms and individuals the ability to import foreign goods, especially luxury items such as expensive automobiles, in order to promote similar, if less well made, Japanese products instead. While the pre-war Japanese gentleman might have been able to drive a Lincoln or a Cadillac, his postwar counterpart had to drive an inferior version Toyota or Nissan; at the same time, there were more Japanese who could afford to buy these because the benefits of economic growth now remained in Japan.

As economic growth progressed, however, it became more difficult to exercise direct control over a complex economy, so there was a shift to more monitoring and the exercise of 'administrative guidance' by bureaucrats who threatened to use their powers more often than they invoked them overtly.[4] The early 1960s also saw the rise of former bureaucrats as leading politicians, which added another, more subtle dimension to bureaucratic influence in Japan. Kishi, as already noted, was a former bureaucrat, though his turbulent tenure in office did little to promote the idea of bureaucrats as good politicians. The 1960s, however, were dominated by two other Prime

Ministers who were both former bureaucrats turned politicians: Ikeda, and his successor, Eisaku Sato. Both men were closely associated with the Yoshida school of politicians which itself had a strong bureaucratic bias.

It is not unusual to make a distinction between party politicians and former bureaucrats when discussing the leadership of the Liberal Democratic Party: bureaucrats were powerful and respected, while politicians were at best tolerated as a necessary evil. It is true that party politicians were on average less well educated than their bureaucratic counterparts and more likely to have a strong regional accent. Moreover, former bureaucrats would also have valuable policy knowledge in the areas covered by the agencies or ministries in which they had worked, a knowledge which politicians often lacked. At the same time, party politicians such as Tanaka were useful – even influential – in their ability to manage political conflict within the party, relations with the opposition parties and public opinion. Tanaka worked well with both Ikeda and Sato, and though he was associated with the Sato faction, he advanced under Ikeda as much as under Sato.

Even so, party politicians such as Tanaka were still viewed disdainfully by members of the elite, including many bureaucrats. In 1961, for example, Tanaka was expressly not invited to join a club begun for Japan's up-and-coming young leaders born in the Taisho era (1911–25) called the Taisho Association which included prominent politicians (such as Yasuhiro Nakasone), financiers (such as Noboru Goto), authors (Yukio Mishima), actors (Toshiro Mifune) and scholars (Kentaro Hayashi) and met once a month in an exclusive Japanese-style restaurant (*ryotei*), 'Kanetanaka', in the Shinbashi district of Tokyo. A professor from Meiji University, Hirotatsu Fujiwara, asked the other members why Tanaka had not been invited. After all, Tanaka had been born in 1918 and became Minister of Posts and Telecommunications at the exceptionally young age of 39, which one would have thought qualified him for membership. However, as Fujiwara points out:

> Immediately after his appointment, he began to appear on commercial radio programs bellowing out *naniwa-bushi* (traditional Japanese folk ballads) and issued numerous licences for new commercial broadcasting companies which made him quite a topic of conversation. Yet, in the eyes of Taisho Association members at the time, however, he was viewed as a parvenu rustic building contractor and there was no question of his becoming a member.[5]

Despite such views among Japan's elite, Tanaka continued to grow in stature. In July 1961 he was appointed chairman of the Political Affairs Research Committee (PARC) of the LDP, one of the three most important posts in the party. PARC had and still has primary responsibility for reviewing policies and legislation, acting in effect as a parallel bureaucracy to the Japanese government. At this crucial period in the development of the Japanese economy, Tanaka ensured that LDP policies would promote growth. His success in this post, one of the most important and coveted posts in the party, qualified him for the even more prestigious position of Finance Minister.

. . .

FINANCIAL CRISIS

Tanaka's crucial role in the Japanese economy became glaringly obvious during his tenure as Finance Minister for four terms, or nearly three years, between July 1962 and June 1965. He won the respect of the bureaucrats in the Ministry of Finance, the cream of the Japanese bureaucratic elite, but he also took decisive action on his own to avert a financial crisis. His experiences in this crucial ministry had long-term consequences for Japan, particularly the Japanese economy.

In a typical exhibition of false modesty after he was appointed Finance Minister and had assembled ministry officials, Tanaka claimed: 'You are the elite of the elite. No one can match your intelligence. Accordingly, I will leave the thinking to you.'[6] It was easy enough for the bureaucrats to believe him, because, unless they were themselves former bureaucrats, most party politicians in reality left the bureaucrats to themselves. Tanaka was merely reinforcing the stereotype as well as reassuring those who had heard of his deep involvement in policy. However, Tanaka was never content to leave the bureaucrats alone.

Tanaka had spent his career cultivating bureaucrats and no ministry was more important than the Ministry of Finance (MOF). The ministry controlled the Fiscal Investment and Loan Programme which invested massive government funds and played a major role in supplying capital to industry to make the economic miracle possible. It also played a central role in the regulation of financial services including banks, insurance companies and stock brokerage firms. With the Bank of Japan, MOF also determined Japan's monetary policy, which assured that low-cost capital was made available for business to invest for growth. The most important power of the Ministry of Finance, however, was its responsibility for determining the amount of government budget to be allocated to competing spending priorities.

At first, Tanaka had the impression that MOF bureaucrats were treating him as if he were an idiot, but he eventually won them over with a combination of acumen and rewards. An example of acumen, although he angered many in the ministry, was his announcement to the press of the size of the first budget for which he was responsible, even before the bureaucrats had finished compiling government spending plans and estimating government revenue, and in fact the actual budget was very close to Tanaka's original estimate. He was amazingly astute with figures and had a good sense of spending needs and priorities. This episode among others led to his nickname, 'the computerised bulldozer'.[7] Not only was he as fast and accurate as a computer, but he also bulldozed ahead through opposition to achieve his goals.

With regard to rewards, Tanaka was quite open about his ability to manipulate MOF bureaucrats. He is quoted as saying:

> The bureaucrat is an animal who, all things considered, wants only to obtain higher rank. The guys who think not of themselves but of Japan go only as far as section chief in this Ministry. Now, those who move from department head to bureau chief or to vice minister cannot oppose what the Minister says. I give them a little pocket money, a promotion, or perhaps take them out somewhere nice. If they want to stand for election, I help them out. And if I take care of things for them in this way, they will keep in line.[8]

No doubt MOF officials also enjoyed the general feel-good factor of the early 1960s' economic boom in Japan. However, such periods of high growth led some to ignore the risk of an economic downturn. The first major crisis of the period occurred in 1965. The problem was that in the years leading up to the 1965 financial crisis, 'The major Japanese brokerage firms were issuing attractive, 6 per cent bonds to individuals, then taking this money and plunging it into the stock market on their own account. Yamaichi securities was especially aggressive in using individual clients' money for purchasing stock of their favoured, publicly quoted corporate clients, to shore up their declining shares.'[9]

Brokerage firms could have turned to the major banks for funds to cover customer redemption of their bonds, but the banks were not allowed to loan money to stockbrokers, as a result of the separation of financial services made during the Occupation *zaibatsu* dissolution reforms. The Ministry of Finance was the only body that could authorise any bank, including the Bank of Japan, to make loans to the foundering firms. The Ministry of Finance was reluctant to bail out an industry which they regarded as no more than respectable gambling. As the market continued to decline, however, the need for funds to shore up the brokerage companies became urgent. On the morning of 21 May 1965, the news that the Yamaichi was about to collapse became public, and in the ensuing panic it was feared that other firms would fall as well. At 11:30, Tanaka held a press conference to reassure investors: 'The Bank of Japan is prepared to lend money to Yamaichi if necessary.'[10]

Alletzhauser expresses the drama of the subsequent confrontation between Tanaka and the Japanese economic establishment most succinctly:

> After the press conference, the Bank of Japan issued a statement expressing the Bank's reservations on lending money to Yamaichi Securities. By noon, pandemonium had broken out in each of Yamaichi's ninety branches . . . Officials from the Bank of Japan, Fuji Bank, Mitsubishi Bank, Industrial Bank of Japan and the Ministry of Finance gathered after the stockmarket close on 28 May to decide how to stem investor panic. 'Let us be careful' the president of Mitsubishi Bank remarked. Tanaka, the Minister of Finance, got angry: 'You call yourself the president of a bank?' Shortly thereafter, at the instigation of Tanaka, all parties agreed to tell the press that the government was prepared to lend an unlimited amount to save Yamaichi and the Japanese securities industry. On 7 June, the Bank of Japan agreed to lend Yamaichi 28 billion yen and Oi Securities 5.3 billion yen, withholding from the public that they would also lend vast sums to other impoverished stock houses.[11]

One of the directors of a major securities firm at the time believed that the industry would have collapsed without the infusion of cash and that 'the decision by Tanaka to lend freely and willingly to brokers was not an obvious one. "The Japanese financial world would be a lot different if Tanaka had not forced the Bank of Japan to lend money." Everyone but Tanaka was fighting to prevent money being lent to the brokers, men whom they considered financial parasites.'[12]

After Tanaka's bailout of the brokerage industry, the belief that the government would never allow a major financial institution to collapse became firmly entrenched. This boosted investor confidence and secured the highly leveraged form of corporate financing which helped to make cheap capital available to Japanese firms. By November 1965, the Japanese economy had begun to grow at high levels again at the beginning of an economic boom that would last an unprecedented 56 months. Tanaka had kept the miracle alive, but he had also sown the seeds of long-term overconfidence in the financial sector in Japan which would harm Japan well after he had gone.

. . .

DUBIOUS DEALS

The success of the Japanese economy also translated into direct personal gains for Tanaka. By the early 1960s, Tanaka was an informal paid advisor (*komon*) to several companies, including Imperial Oil, one of Japan's larger petroleum companies. However, Tanaka's most notorious business dealings began with his involvement with the construction firm Nihon Denken. In 1959, the owner of the company, who had fully controlled the company's shares, died and the newly-appointed chairman of the board of directors eventually brought in Tanaka, who became president of the firm in 1961.

Nihon Denken was a housing construction firm which built houses by relying on monthly payments from prospective homeowners and as a result had a large fund of homeowner capital. Tanaka changed the nature of the firm by using the capital and unsold land – other people's money and assets – as collateral to speculate in real estate and the stock market. At the same time, Tanaka created ghost companies, nominally run by relatives, to hold his personal assets, including a taxi company in Niigata and his large home in Meijiro in Tokyo. All these companies were involved in a variety of deals producing enormous profits based on inside information which Tanaka could have obtained as a public official. These business activities were questionable at best, but not clearly illegal at the time.

For example, as chairman of the Water Resource Development Committee of the Lower House of the Japanese parliament in the late 1950s, Tanaka managed deliberations on the major flood control and river management projects planned by the government, and as Minister of Finance he was also in a position to control sales of government land. It is true that he resigned as president of Nihon Denken and other firms, but this did not prevent the companies which he had created from taking advantage of several lucrative government land deals in the early to mid-1960s. One of his ghost companies, Muromachi Industries, bought the river bed rights to the Shinano River which was scheduled to be part of a major dam project in Niigata and sold land at a great profit for the siting of the Kashiwazaki nuclear power plant, also in his home prefecture. In addition, Tanaka's companies earned massive profits as a result of deals to inflate the price of land at Koumyougaike and Toriyanogata in Niigata, and gained suspiciously from the siting of Niigata University.

It was not only Tanaka, but also Tanaka's associates who gained from many of these deals. Kenji Osano, a Japanese national who purchased the Princess Kaiulani Hotel in Hawaii in 1963 at a time when foreign exchange was jealously controlled by the government, was an associate of Tanaka who twice seems to have benefited from his relationship with the Finance Minister. When Osano needed an urgent release of foreign exchange for another land deal overseas, the approval not only came but came with unusual speed. In addition, the Ministry of Finance approved a sale of government land in the central Toranomon area of Tokyo from which Osano earned 2.7 billion yen in profits. Four months later, when Tanaka's company Nihon Denken was in trouble and putting him in an embarrassing position, Osana bought the company by paying 160 yen for shares that were valued at only 50 yen each in what appeared to be a pay off to Tanaka.[13]

The evidence for Tanaka's involvement in wrongdoing is circumstantial but persuasive, and is supported by the fact that Tanaka's sales of public land during his tenure as Finance Minister, for example, far outstripped that of his predecessors and successors, some by as much as six times.[14] Tanaka was not alone in his dubious dealings, but his activities added to a general atmosphere of corruption in the mid-1960s which grew thicker with the rise of his faction leader, Eisaku Sato, to the premiership.

. . .

DEALING WITH THE OPPOSITION

Few would have imagined that Sato, who became Prime Minister in 1965, would achieve a record for the longest term of office which stands to this day. Some of the credit for this achievement must go to Tanaka, who had become Sato's right-hand man in the party when he was shifted from the Finance Ministry to the sensitive job of LDP party secretary. Sato was known for his skill in managing the difficult task of balancing the demands of the various forces within the Liberal Democratic Party, but he was also lucky that the timely death of two of his main rivals, Bamboku Ono and Ichiro Kono, eliminated key sources of potential internal party opposition.[15]

External opposition, however, was a formidable threat. Sato came to power with a right-wing reputation, facing two major issues: the Japanese response to the International Labour Organization (ILO)'s criticisms of Japanese labour practices and normalisation of relations with South Korea. On both issues the LDP was facing serious opposition from the main opposition party, the Socialists, who were backed by organised labour and who had strong sympathies with North Korea's position on the unification of the Korean peninsula. The Socialists were expected to use all the tactics of parliamentary obstruction at their disposal on both these issues.

One forum which the parties have always had to manage their conflict in parliament in is the Parliamentary Affairs Committee, to which each party sends a representative. If a compromise agreement can be reached in the committee then disruption to the normal business of government can be minimised, but reaching an accord can be a sensitive process. Threats are exchanged and concessions have to be made. At the same time, the negotiations are conducted in both formal and informal settings. One of the tools used by the LDP was to spend small amounts of money to pay for meetings at exclusive restaurants (*ryotei*) at which discussion could be undertaken in a less confrontational atmosphere.

The data for LDP spending on parliamentary affairs in 1965 in the midst of deliberations on the ILO response and South Korean normalisation reveals much about the use of the funds and the way in which Tanaka approached the task. For the first six months of 1965, Takeo Miki was the party secretary and Hideo Sato was LDP parliamentary affairs chairman. Small amounts were spent initially (500,000 yen), but once the opposition made a concession and allowed deliberations to progress, larger sums were disbursed (between 1 million and 5.1 million yen). As soon as Tanaka became party secretary in June 1965, the amounts used on parliamentary affairs by the LDP doubled on average almost immediately. By the end of the year, when South Korea normalisation legislation was finally passed, Tanaka and his parliamentary affairs chairman, Shiro Nakano, spent over 80 million yen in just one month.[16]

It has often been alleged that opposition politicians took direct cash payments from Tanaka or his protégés in return for softening their stance against legislation. Yet even 'normal' *ryotei* politics is a questionable practice. Such elite restaurants supply expensive food and outstanding service, but they may also provide entertainment including *geisha*. One has to be careful not to assume that *geisha* are merely high-class prostitutes. Most have a real skill in traditional Japanese dance or instruments, and all are outstanding conversationalists with a knowledge of games to keep their clients amused. Some *geisha* have acted as glorified prostitutes in many rural inns – at one such inn in Niigata Tanaka himself admitted in his autobiography that he slept with a *geisha* when he was celebrating the opening of his first office at the age of 19 – but high-status *geisha* are usually taken on as mistresses only by the rich and powerful. Tanaka did keep a *geisha* from the Kagurazaka district of Tokyo with whom he had two illegitimate daughters whom he legally recognised, such was the status attached to the relationship. But most MPs, especially in the opposition, were not financially able to maintain a *geisha*. This made them appreciate even more the meals, *geisha* entertainment, gifts, and even sexual favours they received courtesy of Liberal Democratic Party parliamentary affairs funding.

It was within this context that a series of scandals, the so-called Black Mist scandals, began to plague the Sato administration. These involved, among other things, dubious sales of government land, manipulation of the national railroad time table to the benefit of the district of the Transport Minister, and misuse of government funds for private travel. Tanaka was not directly implicated in any of these cases but his behaviour as always contributed to the general atmosphere of wrongdoing which tainted the Sato administration.

There is no doubt that Sato knew what Tanaka was doing.[17] Tanaka was a highly effective manager of the opposition in a period in which it appeared to be a serious threat. The final confirmation of Tanaka's abilities was that the 1966 election, held in the aftermath of the Black Mist controversy, was considered a victory even though the number of LDP seats in parliament fell from 294 out of 486 to 280 (or from 63 to 57.7 per cent). The LDP had expected to do worse, but not only did they maintain a solid majority, their main rivals, the Socialists, also lost three seats.[18]

. . .

URBANISATION, POLITICS AND URBAN POLICY

The Socialists' loss of seats was a big surprise because a common argument made by political analysts in the late 1950s and early 1960s was that the Liberal Democratic Party would inevitably decline and the Socialist Party would move closer to a majority as urbanisation progressed along with economic growth.[19] The Socialists were the most popular party in urban areas in the 1950s and it seemed natural that economic growth would continue to promote the growth of cities along with the depopulation of rural areas so that the Socialist electoral base would eventually outstrip that of the Liberal Democrats. A look at the trends in voting between 1960 and 1969 (see Table 1) confirms that the LDP did indeed decline electorally over the decade as the opposition vote increased, primarily in urban areas.

The beneficiary of urbanisation was not the Japan Socialist Party, however. The Japan Communist Party, which had only one seat in the late 1950s, renounced its early policy of immediate violent revolution and appealed to the urban poor in a way that the Socialists,

Table 1 Support for Japanese political parties, 1960–9

| Party | Elections | | | | | | | |
| | 1960 | | 1963 | | 1967 | | 1969 | |
	Seats/Votes		Seats/Votes		Seats/Votes		Seats/Votes	
LDP	63.2	58.09	63.0	56.01	57.6	49.16	61.7	49.07
DSP	3.6	8.77	4.9	7.37	6.2	7.40	6.4	7.86
KMT	—	—	—	—	5.1	5.38	9.7	10.91
JSP	30.8	27.43	30.8	29.03	29.0	28.04	18.5	21.44
JCP	0.6	2.93	1.1	4.01	1.0	4.67	2.9	6.81

Source: Masumi Ishikawa, *Sengo Nihon Seiji Shi* (1994)
LDP = Liberal Democratic Party; DSP = Democratic Socialist Party; KMT = *Komeito*; JSP = Japan Socialist Party; JCP = Japan Communist Party.

heavily reliant on organised labour, were unable to match. More importantly, one of the major new Buddhist religious sects of the postwar period, *Sokagakkai*, formed its own political party in 1964 and attracted the votes of opposition voters who favoured socialism but were uncomfortable with godless Marxism. With the growth of the Communists and the *Sokagakkai*-backed 'Clean Government Party' (*Komeito*), the Socialists declined alongside their opponents, the Liberal Democrats.

However, there were politicians, such as Tanaka, who were responsive and flexible to the needs of constituents in a way that the opposition, ideologically rigid and without access to government resources, were unable to match. The LDP was certainly a minority in the major cities of Japan, but under the multi-member constituency system used for elections to parliament, the LDP could be assured of at least one seat in urban areas. Even if it did not abandon key constituencies, such as farmers or big business, it did try to appease urban critics enough to hold on to power. Indeed, the LDP did not need to abandon anyone. Policies that were inclusive and responsive to voter demands, as typified by the Tanaka approach to politics, could co-opt urban constituencies as well as rural constituencies.

For the brief period in the late 1960s when Tanaka was temporarily out of the political spotlight, he applied himself to managing the problems of Japan's urban areas with the same determination and creativity he had shown in other areas. He was made the chairman of the Urban Policy Commission in March 1967 which resulted in the publication of the Outline of Urban Policy in April 1968. The document constituted a thorough investigation of Japan's land use policies and made several radical recommendations concerning further land policy.[20]

It also demonstrated that Tanaka was sensitive to the gains being made by the opposition in urban areas and the need to do something to respond. It was not a natural reaction for conservative politicians, most of whom were primarily oriented toward their rural constituencies. Tanaka, however, did not ignore any possible area where new policies could create benefits for the average Japanese and increased support for Tanaka and his party. It is significant that the ideas expressed in these reports eventually became the core of a best-selling book which appeared just as he was attempting to run for the leadership of the Liberal Democratic Party and become Prime Minister.

. . .
POLITICAL MENTOR

As infighting on the left in the late 1960s helped to neutralise both the Socialists and the Communists, and student radicalism sent shock waves through both left parties as much as the rest of Japanese society, only the Buddhist *Komeito* appeared to be (and believed itself to be) unstoppable. As the religious group *Sokagakkai* which backed the *Komeito* continued to gain believers, it grew in confidence and became a political force which could not be ignored. Tanaka's attempts to come to terms with the *Komeito* were just the start of a long-term relationship between the LDP and the *Komeito* which continues today, but the relationship between Tanaka and the *Komeito* was hardly noticed at first.

Exposure of Tanaka's involvement with the *Komeito* began when a Meiji University professor, Hirotatsu Fujiwara, who was about to publish a book critical of *Sokagakkai*, the parent organisation of the *Komeito*, began to receive pressure from the organisation to stop the book coming out. Some of the pressure came in the form of thinly veiled threats ('you had better watch out, there have been a lot of traffic accidents'),[21] but ultimately, Tanaka became involved in a more subtle campaign to persuade Fujiwara to suspend publication. The incident provides insights into Tanaka's relationship with the *Komeito* as well as his general thought and tactics which, though more subtle than threats, were just as dubious.

During the morning of 4 October 1969, Fujiwara received an unexpected telephone call from Tanaka. Tanaka asked Fujiwara if something could be done about the book, admitting that *Komeito* chairman Takeire had asked him to persuade Fujiwara to do something to stop or at least limit publication.[22] While Fujiwara insisted it was impossible for him to back down as it was a matter of freedom of speech, Tanaka replied that he was merely interested in making a deal. Tanaka admitted it would be to his political advantage to do favours for the *Komeito* because as a politician without a bureaucratic background he needed all the support he could get.[23] Tanaka's proposal was for Fujiwara to agree to put out a first edition, distribute a handful of copies to those immediately interested, and then the *Komeito* would buy up the rest of the copies so that Fujiwara would be guaranteed a profit but the damage to the *Komeito* would be minimised.

Fujiwara agreed to meet with Tanaka at the *ryotei* called 'Chiyoshin', but there too Fujiwara argued that a deal was not acceptable due to the principles involved. In fact, Fujiwara was offended at the very idea of limiting the freedom of the press: '"This is an outrageous conversation"', he remarked in disgust. Fujiwara continues: 'When Tanaka heard this, he expressed surprise. He seemed to want to tell me that I was a fool not to accept such good terms', but [Tanaka] merely said, '"OK I understand. What it amounts to is that by asking this of you, I will make myself indebted to you. If you grant this difficult favour for me, I will never forget it. I will undertake without conditions however difficult a task which you might ask of me later" with a confidence that any political commentator or journalist could be bought with the right type of bribe.'[24]

That was the end of the meeting as far as Fujiwara was concerned. Tanaka said he would phone again about the next time and place to discuss the matter. When Fujiwara appeared for a second meeting at the *ryotei* 'Nobu Nakagawa', Tanaka assumed that he had decided to accept the offer. Places were set for six at the table with Tanaka expecting a celebratory meal with all involved. When Fujiwara read out a prepared statement insisting on his right to freedom of speech, Tanaka stalled by making small talk in anticipation of a telephone call, presumably from the others who were to join them. Tanaka returned from the phone conversation and announced that negotiations were over. Finally, Fujiwara admonished Tanaka for becoming involved when he was planning to run for prime minister one day, but Tanaka merely glared at Fujiwara and broke out in a sweat in response.[25] While Fujiwara had been in discussions with Tanaka, harassment and threats had stopped. After this final meeting, however, Fujiwara's problems continued with Tanaka himself playing a minor role in harassing him.[26]

Fujiwara tried to make an issue of Tanaka's involvement. At first, he tried to persuade Sato to drop Tanaka, but it was clear that Tanaka did Sato's dirty work and was too useful to abandon. In the end, Fujiwara had to rely on the Communist Party to raise the issue in parliament, which discredited his arguments in the eyes of many. It is surprising that Tanaka should have embroiled himself in such a potentially damaging affair, and Fujiwara speculates that Tanaka was being blackmailed. Even so, a less sinister explanation is more likely. Tanaka had befriended the *Komeito* leader, Takeire; as he told Fujiwara: '[Takeire] is not the frightening fascist you make him out to be. He may be politically immature, but I've been working as his political coach. He's happy if I'm kind to him so I have been teaching him some things.'[27] There were definite advantages for Tanaka in having a co-operative relationship with the *Komeito*.

In fact, Tanaka had developed a good working relationship with all the political parties with the exception of the Communists and a handful of left Socialists. By the beginning of the 1970s, Tanaka was again party secretary and was able to deal with challenges to the LDP on several fronts. The Vietnam War was becoming more intense; radical students in Japan had shut down the major Japanese university and were promising a repeat of the protests over the US–Japan Security Treaty when it came to be renewed automatically in 1970. The opposition parties were growing in strength as the problems of high economic growth began to emerge, particularly the issues of pollution control and social welfare. In addition, trade disputes with the United States started to become serious. Yet he managed to help to lead the LDP to a moral victory in the 1969 general election in which they had been expected to lose power, and when he ended his final stint as party secretary in 1971, he was even given a farewell party by the opposition – an unprecedented event for a conservative politician.[28]

. . .

CONSTITUENCY SERVICE

As Tanaka grew increasingly prominent at the national level, he nonetheless still took care of his own constituency, and his efforts in the high-growth decade were directed at enriching his own constituency as much as himself:

> He promised his constituents he would double-track the local rail road, and by 1967 he did. Never satisfied, he promised them a bullet train as well. Thanks largely to his bureaucratic influence, the state-owned rail road authority then laid 300 kilometres of the wide-gauge track to take the bullet train into his district, dug 103 kilometres of tunnels, and built five special stations, all at a cost of 480 billion yen. As [Finance] Minister and senior LDP statesman, Tanaka increased the subsidies to his prefecture from 12.1 billion yen in 1962 to 24.1 billion yen in 1965 and 53.3 billion yen in 1970. By the time he became Prime Minister in 1972, he raised subsidies to 80.6 billion.[29]

The construction projects benefited local firms as well as the big national firms who captured the major public works construction contracts.[30] Major firms often subcontracted segments of the work to well-connected local firms. Moreover, Tanaka's policies led to a plethora of minor public works contracts of which local firms might take advantage. For example, when he was Finance Minister, Tanaka had the government define heavy snow as a natural disaster in addition to previously accepted disasters such as flood, earthquake and fire. As such, a heavy snowfall qualified for government assistance both in emergency aid to those affected and in public works projects to prevent avalanches and other problems associated with snowbound regions such as Niigata. This policy initiative opened up a steady stream of government contracts which benefited local construction firms in Niigata and elsewhere.

Control of patronage on this scale soon translated into a dominating presence for Tanaka in Niigata politics. He effectively appointed the prefectural governor of Niigata in 1961 and maintained an influence at every level of the prefecture, both within his own district and in neighbouring areas.[31] These activities did occasionally get him into trouble. For example, in 1955 it was alleged that funds from Tanaka's Nagaoka Railroad Company had been used to bribe local assembly members in the Niigata prefectural assembly. The problem was compounded by sloppy bookkeeping which made it difficult to know who in the company was at fault or where the money went, and though Tanaka was nominally responsible as head of the firm, no charges were brought.[32]

Tanaka was also extending his influence beyond Niigata as he used his position as party secretary during the 1969 general election to cultivate a group of 13 MPs who would eventually form the core of his faction and influence Japanese politics long after Tanaka had left the political scene. These included Ichiro Ozawa, Tsutomu Hata and Seiroku Kajiyama. Many of these individuals were second-generation MPs who took over their fathers' *koenkai* and used them as bases on which to build safe seats. Tanaka knew how to pick winners, and second-generation MPs were a good bet. Tanaka made them indebted to him, promoted them and relied on them to do his bidding. Part of their task was to recruit faction members at the local level in prefectural and city assemblies in their own districts. In doing so, the Tanaka faction extended its influence to a depth unrivalled by any other faction.

. . .

CONCLUSION

In the 1960s, Tanaka's 'constituency' was widening beyond Niigata. Opposition parties liked him, bureaucrats helped him and general respect for his abilities grew in the LDP and the public at large. While he was not always successful, his record of 'getting things done' was impressive and he was a key player in the creation of the Japanese miracle. Bureaucrats were important in Japan, but so were politicians, especially men like Tanaka who at crucial times could achieve political compromises in ways with which more squeamish members of the elite were loath to associate themselves.

Tanaka saved the financial system and co-opted key elements of the opposition while creating the basis for co-opting the opposition's constituency as well. Economic growth hurt the LDP but it also hurt their rivals the Socialists, and thanks to Tanaka, the LDP appeared better able to respond effectively to the new situation. Tanaka had gone from being a disdained upstart to one of the central politicians in Japan. In the early 1970s, Tanaka would extend his approach even further, with serious long-term consequences for Japan.

. . .

NOTES AND REFERENCES

1 Edward Lincoln, *Japan: Facing Economic Maturity* (Washington, DC, 1988), p. 3.
2 Robert Evans Jr, 'Japan's Economy: An Economist's View', *The Japan Foundation Newsletter*, vol. 17, no. 3 (Dec. 1989).
3 Edward Denison and William Chung, 'Economic Growth and Its Sources', in Hugh Partick and Henry Rosovsky (eds), *Asia's New Giant: How the Japanese Economy Works* (Washington, DC, 1976), pp. 101–5.
4 Chalmers Johnson, *MITI and the Japanese Miracle* (Stanford, CA, 1982), pp. 242–74.
5 Hirotatsu Fujiwara, trans. John Clark, *Tanaka Kakuei: Godfather of Japan* (1985), pp. 170–3.
6 Quoted in Albert Craig, 'Functional and Dysfunctional Aspects of Government Bureaucracy', in Ezra F. Vogel (ed.), *Modern Japanese Organization and Decision-making* (1975), p. 29.
7 Yoh Mizuki, *Tanaka Kakuei: Sono Kyozen to Kyoaku* [Kakuei Tanaka: His Greatness and Wickedness] (1998), p. 115.

8 Fujiwara, *Tanaka Kakuei: Godfather of Japan*, p. 204.
9 Al Alletzhauser, *The House of Nomura* (London, 1990), p. 156.
10 *Ibid.*, p. 159.
11 *Ibid.*, p. 160.
12 *Ibid.*, p. 161.
13 Takashi Tachibana, *Tanaka Kakuei Kenkyu Zenkiryoku* [A Study of Kakuei Tanaka: The Full Record] (1982), vol. 1, p. 87.
14 *Ibid.*, pp. 85–7.
15 Masumi Ishikawa, *Deeta Sengo Seiji Shi* [Postwar Political History with Data] (1984), p. 72.
16 Gendai Seiji Mondai Kenkyukai (ed.), *Jiminto Giwaku Shi* [History of LDP Scandal] (1979), pp. 293–5.
17 Takao Iwami, *Tanaka Kakuei: Seiji no Tensai* [Kakuei Tanaka: Political Genius] (1999), p. 110.
18 Ishikawa, *Deeta Sengo Seiji Shi*, p. 74.
19 For example, see Hirohide Ishida, 'Hoshu Seito no Bishon' [Vision for the Conservative Party], *Chuo Koron*, cited in Kent Calder, *Crisis and Compensation: Public Policy and Political Stability in Japan, 1949–1986* (Princeton, NJ, 1988), pp. 100–1.
20 Shiro Nakano, *Tanaka Seiken: 886 Hi* [The Tanaka Administration: 886 Days] (1982), pp. 300–8.
21 Fujiwara, *Tanaka Kakuei: Godfather of Japan*, p. 62.
22 *Ibid.*, p. 38.
23 *Ibid.*, p. 67.
24 *Ibid.*, pp. 69–70.
25 *Ibid.*, p. 72.
26 *Ibid.*, p. 162.
27 *Ibid.*, pp. 66–8.
28 Niigata Nippo Hodobu, *Tanaka Kakuei, Rongu Guddobai* [Kakuei Tanaka: Long Goodbye] (Niigata, 1995), p. 162.
29 J.M. Ramseyer and F. Rosenbluth, *Japan's Political Marketplace* (Cambridge, MA, 1993), pp. 122–3.
30 Niigata Nippo Hodobu, *Tanaka Kakuei, Rongu Guddobai*, pp. 59–60.
31 *Ibid.*, pp. 55–6.
32 Tachibana, *Tanaka Kakuei Kenkyu*, vol. 1, pp. 71–2.

Chapter 5

TANAKA IN POWER

Tanaka had been very helpful to Sato but by the end of the 1960s, it appeared that Sato's long tenure in office was finally going to come to an end. While several faction leaders were eager to replace Sato, one politician turned bureaucrat, Takeo Fukuda, was widely believed to be his heir apparent. In the end, however, Tanaka defeated Fukuda due both to brilliant manoeuvring in the internal politics of the Liberal Democratic Party, and to widespread support for Tanaka as the people's Prime Minister. Tanaka's subsequent policy initiatives did not disappoint party and popular expectations, as radical changes were begun in Japanese domestic priorities at the same time as Tanaka transformed Japan's relations with the outside world.

It is astonishing that Tanaka became Prime Minister at all given that he faced the formidable obstacle of Takeo Fukuda as Sato's heir apparent. Fukuda's background suggested clear advantages over someone like Tanaka. Fukuda had been born into a well-off landlord's family, attended a good school and entered the prestigious University of Tokyo law faculty. While still at university he took the examination for the Ministry of Finance and passed with top marks. After rising steadily to the top in the ministry during the war, Fukuda was implicated in a scandal in 1948 under the Socialist–Democratic Party coalition, though, like Tanaka, he was later cleared. With close family members already successful in local politics, it was no surprise that Fukuda was elected to parliament as an independent in 1952. He soon became close to Kishi when Kishi was expelled from the Liberal Party by Yoshida, and, again like Tanaka, he was propelled at a relatively young age to high office in the Kishi administration.

In terms of personality, Fukuda was a strait-laced member of the elite while Tanaka was an outgoing, self-made man. In contrast to

Tanaka's energetic and exuberant style, Fukuda was uncomfortable with the average voter and found election campaigning difficult due to his inability to drink, socialise and generally come down to the same level as the voters in his district.[1] Such important personality differences also came through in both men's relationships with women. In a series of autobiographical articles written for the Wall Street Journal of Japan, the *Nihon Keizai Shimbun*, Fukuda mentions a woman in his life only once, whereas numerous women appear in Tanaka's memoirs.[2]

Those around Tanaka knew well that he had many women friends in the clubs and elite restaurants in the entertainment districts around the parliamentary area of Tokyo known as Nagata-cho – so many, in fact, that he was considered the Casanova of Nagata-cho – and one can see women of every age in the foreground of pictures of his public speaking engagements.[3] As noted earlier, the secretary of the Etsuzankai, Akiko Sato, was his mistress with whom he had a child, and he kept a *geisha* as a mistress with whom he also had two children. Not only did Fukuda lack sex appeal but such passionate behaviour by him was unthinkable.

The problem for Tanaka was that his lack of polish and dubious background damaged his standing with the political and economic establishment. Even Prime Minister Sato clearly preferred Fukuda to Tanaka as successor even though Fukuda led a rival faction to Sato and Tanaka was a loyal senior member of Sato's own faction. Like Sato, Fukuda was a former bureaucrat, and like Sato, he was firmly on the political right. In addition, Fukuda's faction had originally been the faction of Sato's brother, Kishi. Yet, despite his preference for Fukuda, Sato found it difficult to let him take over the reins of power. Fukuda was deeply disappointed when Sato decided to stand for re-election for an unprecedented fourth term which he easily won. Tanaka played on Sato's reluctance to step down by helping to engineer the re-election to buy time for himself to replace Sato.[4] He used the time to create a high profile for himself in the new cabinet as a springboard to a successful candidacy.

. . .

FORAY INTO FOREIGN AFFAIRS

In early July 1971, Sato formed his last cabinet. Fukuda assumed the post of Foreign Minister while Tanaka became Minister for

International Trade and Industry. Almost immediately, the new government was rocked by a serious problem in the form of the so-called 'Nixon Shocks'. First of all, the US announced that President Richard Nixon would visit the People's Republic of China, which was a shock because Japan had been careful not to improve relations with mainland China out of deference to US wishes. Now the US had not only gone ahead with improving its own relations with China, but had not informed Japan of the impending policy change. Then in August, Nixon announced an end to the system of fixed exchange rates which meant that the yen – a cheap currency under the system making it easy to export – surged in value. In addition to the damage of a strong currency, the Nixon administration also added a 15 per cent import surcharge on goods entering the United States which further undermined Japan's competitiveness in its most crucial export market. While these changes were not aimed at Japan alone, Japan felt the full brunt of Nixon's policy shift.

Japan's continuing trade surplus against the US was certainly a major contributory cause of the sense of crisis which induced the Nixon administration to act. It was the beginning of full-scale trade friction which would plague relations between the two countries for years to come. The main focus of the friction at this time was the long-simmering dispute over the level of Japanese textile exports to the United States. The main difference between the textile problem and other potential trade conflicts was that it had important domestic political constituencies in both countries. Local textile manufacturing in Japan was spread among the constituencies of LDP MPs; in the US, textiles were concentrated in Southern states. Since Southern representatives were powerful figures in the US Senate, they had to be appeased, especially as one of the key initiatives of the Sato administration – the return of Okinawa to Japanese control after the US occupation that had been in place since the end of World War II – depended on such senators for ratification. Sato privately agreed to resolve the textile dispute on terms acceptable to the US as part of the price for achieving the return of Okinawa to Japan, though he never made the Japanese government fully aware of the extent of his commitment to the United States.

This situation caused problems for Fukuda given the delicate balance to be maintained by the Foreign Ministry in appeasing US demands while domestic political forces also needed to be considered. On the other hand, it provided an ideal opportunity for Tanaka to gain further prominence. Fukuda, for example, felt compelled to concede publicly that negotiations with the US would have to open, no doubt following the advice of the Foreign Ministry which was eager to maintain good relations with the US. But Tanaka immediately and very visibly contradicted Fukuda by announcing directly to US representatives that there was no evidence of damage to the US textile industry from Japanese exports and that any agreement was politically impossible. Thus, Tanaka took a strong pro-Japanese position while Fukuda came across as appeasing the US.

Tanaka knew that he would eventually have to come to an agreement, but he was determined to appear to be defending Japanese interests. Indeed, Tanaka worked tacitly with US negotiator Kennedy to stage-manage the situation. Kennedy and his subordinates would issue an ultimatum which Tanaka would be seen reluctantly to accept in exchange for some US concessions, relatively minor concessions but concessions nonetheless. In addition, Kennedy and Tanaka agreed to conduct negotiations among only a small group of people to limit the involvement of the Foreign Ministry and to exclude Fukuda from the process.[5]

Aware of the potential political fallout of any settlement favourable to the US, Tanaka also arranged for a generous package of aid to the textile industry to compensate them for any losses associated with the new agreement. The relief package created by Tanaka would guarantee the industry growth and profits despite any limitations on exports. While there was some initial resistance from the bureaucracy, Tanaka was able to call on individual officials in the Ministry of Finance and Ministry of Trade and Industry to find the funds, arrange the details of the plan and make it a workable proposal. The textile industry still remained opposed to the plan but most of big business recognised that the agreement would improve trade relations with the US which would be of greater benefit in the long run, so the plan was accepted. Moreover, Tanaka's approach – tough talk, compromise, compensation, return to good trade relations – set the pattern for trade agreements thereafter.[6]

Both the Okinawa issue and the textile dispute served Tanaka beyond the negotiations themselves. Toward the end of the Okinawa negotiations, a US–Japan summit was held at President Nixon's vacation home in San Clemente, California, early in 1972. In addition to Prime Minister Sato and Fukuda as Foreign Minister, Tanaka was invited along in order to provide an opportunity for Sato to explain to Tanaka that Fukuda was to be Sato's anointed successor. However, Tanaka avoided discussion of the issue and instead used the opportunity to raise his media profile by having himself photographed with the President. For example, at a post-summit White House garden party, Tanaka had Nixon invite him from a separate table to the main table where the President, Sato and Fukuda were seated. Nixon seemed to have a natural affinity with Tanaka, and Tanaka used the implicit endorsement to his advantage. The final blow to Fukuda came when Sato delayed his resignation in order to remain in office long enough to participate in the treaty signing ceremony and the formal return of Okinawa. This gave Tanaka additional time to capitalise on his new prominence and organise an effective challenge to Fukuda.[7]

. . .

BEST-SELLER

Despite this foreign policy success, Tanaka's main strength was domestic policy, and all of his ideas for transforming Japan were drawn together in a book: *Building a New Japan: A Plan for Remodelling the Japanese Archipelago*. In it Tanaka offered a vision of an improved Japan where problems of overcrowding, pollution and industrial competitiveness were solved by a massive restructuring of the country through the relocation of industry out of the existing urban conglomerations such as Tokyo and Osaka to other areas.

The book was not only the culmination of Tanaka's own postwar experience, building on the influence of his pre-war patron, Viscount Okochi, in such matters; it also drew on the network of supporters and clients he had cultivated among regional interest groups, bureaucrats and politicians. The role of MITI bureaucrats as ghost writers is often cited but officials in other agencies also had a hand in the project. Although Tanaka was a prolific writer, he probably did not write the book directly. As Passin notes: 'A popular joke at the time was that, when [Tanaka] heard that his book had become a best seller, he said "I guess if it is so popular, I'll have to buy a copy and read it too." '[8]

The real problem for Tanaka was that the presidency of the Liberal Democratic Party was not a popularity contest decided by the public or even by the wider party membership. Selection depended entirely on the support of a majority of LDP MPs, and most LDP MPs were committed to one faction leader or another. In the 1960s, the Sato faction had been the largest faction with around 100 LDP

MPs from both Houses of the Japanese parliament. Tanaka played a major role in building this factional strength, but towards the end of the Sato administration, when he began to create his own faction, he could not be sure of the support of many of his Sato faction colleagues, who also tended to support at least one other alternative leader. By contrast, before the leadership election Fukuda had the largest faction in the LDP with nearly 100 MPs of his own. Moreover, Fukuda's strong prospects of becoming Prime Minister would attract opportunists to bolster the number of his loyal followers.

The problem for both candidates was that the bulk of MPs were officially committed to neither side, and as a result, there was massive spending on the contest by the candidates. In terms of reported spending, Fukuda spent the most, but Tanaka was not far behind. Of course, it is impossible to judge the amount spent but not reported. There is no doubt, however, that it was by far the most expensive campaign yet for the presidency of the LDP.

Tanaka's funding was pulled together from a variety of sources, legal and illegal. Significantly, he did not have the support of Japan's business elite, which favoured Fukuda. As Gerald Curtis points out:

> Tanaka won the election in spite of big business, and not because of it. Even if, by the election day, many [business leaders] supported Tanaka, or more commonly, adopted an attitude of 'equal distance' (*dokyori*) from Tanaka and Fukuda, this was because they realized the futility of continued support for Fukuda and not because they had changed their minds about whom they would like to see succeed Prime Minister Sato.[9]

Therefore, most of Tanaka's funding came from non-elite business sources or his own funds.[10]

On the spending side, Tanaka kept a careful record of payments to MPs whose support he was soliciting. He noted paying one MP 5 million yen three times or another 5 million yen five times.[11] These were large amounts by any standard. The amounts being distributed in cash could not be said to be the direct purchase of votes since many would already be voting for Tanaka and others who received the money could not be guaranteed to support him. In addition, Tanaka's funds were channelled through other faction leaders, notably Masayoshi Ohira with whom Tanaka seemed to have reached an understanding even though Ohira was also running for the leadership post. It was rumoured that Yasuhiro Nakasone, whose faction

Table 2 Public opinion polls on the popularity of postwar cabinets

Government	Date of Poll	Support	Do Not Support
Katayama	November 1947	25	54
Ashida	March 1948	30	31
Yoshida	October 1949	43	17
Hatoyama	January 1955	40	8
Ishibashi	December 1956	41	11
Kishi	March 1957	33	13
Sato	November 1964	47	14
Tanaka	August 1972	62	10

Source: Shiro Nakano, *Tanaka Seiken 886 Hi* (Gyosei Mondai Kenkyujo, 1982), pp. 42–3.

held the balance of forces in the LDP, received a large payment to support Tanaka.

The vote was close. On the first ballot, Tanaka led with 156 votes and Fukuda was close behind with 150, but since Ohira captured 101 votes and the small faction leader Takeo Miki attracted 69, no candidate had an overall majority so the contest went to a run-off involving Tanaka and Fukuda, the two with the highest number of votes. It was expected that Ohira's votes would shift to Tanaka. The Miki faction was not comfortable with the right-wing Fukuda, but neither did it feel entirely sure about Tanaka. There were also a number of MPs in small factions. In the final tally, Tanaka won an overwhelming victory with 282 against Fukuda's 109.

After this victory, business and the rest of Japan's conservative elite seemed to acquiesce in Tanaka's election in the hope that he could at least reverse the decline in the popularity of the LDP. Initially at least, he did just that. A *Asahi Shimbun* poll taken soon after the formation of his government gave a 62 per cent support rating for his cabinet – the highest since the 58 per cent achieved by Prime Minister Yoshida in 1952 after the signing of the San Francisco Peace Treaty which ended the Allied occupation of Japan.

The amount of money used by both sides in the contest, however, was a portent of things to come. At the time, the former Prime Minister Kishi, now the senior statesman in the party, expressed his fears privately to his eldest daughter, Yoko (who was married to the politician Shintaro Abe). After Fukuda's defeat, she asked her father why he was so opposed to Tanaka, to which he replied: 'Tanaka gets his hands on "hot" money (*yugei no deru yoo na kane*). That type of prime minister cannot help but create a dangerous situation.'[12] Of course, Kishi would be expected to support Fukuda who was his successor as leader of his faction, but such a criticism from a fellow politician who in the past had himself been implicated in serious scandal and had ties to organised crime was significant. It was also prescient.

. . .

FOREIGN POLICY: AN UNEXPECTED FORTE

Given Tanaka's orientation, it is perhaps surprising that his earliest and most memorable accomplishments were in the area of foreign affairs. It might be easy to dismiss these successes in hindsight as inevitable given the shift in US foreign policy to detente in the same period and the groundwork laid by others in Japan, but the speed and decisiveness of Tanaka's initiatives advanced Japan toward an independent international posture more than in any other period prior to the end of the Cold War. Moreover, it is doubtful if any other Japanese politician at the time had the political power and disposition to change Japan's foreign policy in crucial ways.

Tanaka's first move, only weeks after assuming office, was to follow in the footsteps of US President Richard Nixon and raise the status of Japan's relations with the People's Republic of China. It was not a natural step for a conservative Japanese government. The LDP had been a loyal supporter of US anti-communist policy in East Asia and the leading politicians in the party maintained strong links with the Nationalist Chinese from the pre-war period which continued after the Nationalists assumed control of Japan's former colony Taiwan. While a few LDP politicians did favour improved relations with the communist government on mainland China, the most powerful – including Sato and Fukuda – were overwhelmingly sympathetic to the Nationalists' Republic of China.

It is true that some progress had been made in the last days of the Sato administration, but the process had stalled until Tanaka came to power. In addition, the party chairman of the *Komeito* – Takeire – lent his support to the new Prime Minister. The *Komeito*'s relations with Tanaka had been mutually beneficial and the *Komeito* used its own China contacts to the benefit of both parties. Takeire had already made several trips to Beijing to meet with Communist

Party officials and offered to assist Tanaka in negotiations to nor-
malise relations between the PRC and Japan. While Tanaka and his
Foreign Minister, Ohira, did not respond officially to the offer,
Takeire's visit laid the groundwork for Tanaka's own trip a few
weeks later. It was unusual for an opposition politician to play such
a role in Japan[13] but it can be seen as a natural consequence of
Tanaka's political style.

Before travelling to China, Tanaka visited all the surviving past
prime ministers and visited the graves of the deceased postwar
premiers. He arrived in Beijing with Foreign Minister Ohira and
Cabinet Secretary Nikaido to a warm reception from Chinese Prime
Minister Zhou En-lai on the tarmac at the airport. The Chinese did
their best to make the Japanese visitors feel welcome but it was
a stressful time for Tanaka. He told his personal secretary Akiko
Sato that his blood pressure was so high there was blood in his urine
and he found it so difficult to eat that he could only eat rice gruel
despite the sumptuous banquet prepared for him.[14] He was very
impressed with Zhou, but seemed to have more trouble with Mao
with whom he had only the most superficial conversation.[15]

A joint communiqué agreed by Tanaka and Zhou was signed on
29 September 1972. It avoided the areas of conflict between the two
countries by skilful wording in which a variety of outstanding issues
were left unresolved. Moreover, it was not a legally binding agreement. Nevertheless, it did create a foundation for further progress
in the improvement of bilateral relations. It was not simply a natural
development following the Nixon China visit and the desire of China
for improved relations with the West. As one scholar has put it:

> The successful summitry was a tribute both to Tanaka's political
> decisiveness and to [Zhou's] diplomatic skill. Even though the com-
> bined effects of external stimuli, party politics, business pressure, and
> public mood determined much of his foreign policy outlook, it was
> after all Tanaka's characteristic decisiveness that set the timing and
> pace for resolving Japan's major postwar diplomatic dilemma – a
> dilemma that his predecessors, from Yoshida and Hatoyama to Ikeda
> and Sato, had been unwilling or unable to deal with.[16]

Tanaka followed his performance in Beijing with a visit to Mos-
cow to negotiate improved relations with the Soviet Union. However, his reception from Brezhnev was chilly and talks progressed
slowly. The main sticking point between the two countries was the
Soviet occupation of a small group of islands just north of the

Japanese island of Hokkaido. The Japanese insisted that the return of the territories was a prerequisite to any peace treaty, but the Soviets stressed that the boundaries which had been set as a result of World War II could not be changed and refused even to talk about the issue. The two leaders did manage to hammer out plans for joint development projects of paper and pulp and natural gas and oil in Siberia, and in the end, Tanaka was able to have a few phrases on the Northern Territories inserted into the joint statement which subsequent negotiators found useful.[17]

Characteristically, Tanaka is alleged to have offered to buy the island from the Soviets. 'After all,' he is supposed to have argued, 'Russia sold Alaska to the United States', a remark which his critics argued showed that he thought all problems could be solved with money.[18] Whatever his methods, Tanaka was able to make progress where others had consistently failed. His administration saw the greatest improvement in Sino-Soviet relations of any postwar administration.

Tanaka's main focus was often, as in the Soviet Union, on resource diplomacy. Japan was poor in natural resources and extremely dependent on foreign energy supplies. Much of Tanaka's extensive foreign travel involved a focus on energy supplies. This included Australia and France where uranium supplies and nuclear energy co-operation were discussed. He visited South-east Asia where he faced anti-Japanese riots due to growing Japanese economic hegemony over the region, although he also made progress on securing petroleum supplies from oil-rich Indonesia.

Resource diplomacy was given added impetus by the Arab oil embargo of 1973. 'In these circumstances the Japanese government (the Tanaka cabinet) reacted uncharacteristically quickly to Arab demands by issuing a communiqué delivered by the then Cabinet Secretary Susumu Nikaido, on 22 November 1973.'[19] The communiqué, which urged Israel to withdraw from the territories it had occupied as a result of the 1967 Arab–Israeli war and stressed the right of the Palestinian people to self-determination, was seen as a significant change in Japanese policy, not so much because it responded to Arab demands – it did not fully meet any of them – but because Japan had taken an independent stance in foreign affairs and moved away from the United States' position.[20] Again, it is inconceivable that a Japanese government leader before or after Tanaka would have had the political will to defy the United States on such an issue.

. . .
DOMESTIC VISION

With dramatic international events occupying centre stage, it is easy to forget the impact which Tanaka also had on domestic policy. Indeed, it is for foreign policy that the Tanaka government is often best remembered in Japan, with one treatment of his administration devoting 220 out of 370 pages to his foreign policy activities. However, as Gerald Curtis points out, Tanaka's domestic policy was no less energetically pursued:

> Within a few years, and mainly under Tanaka's leadership, the LDP sponsored legislation that replaced the previous hands-off government attitude toward industrial pollution with a package of the most stringent pollution control measures imposed by any country. Then in 1973, in what was typed 'welfare's birthyear' (*fukushi gannen*), Tanaka introduced an upgraded social security pension system and expanded low-cost health care under the national health insurance system.[21]

Moreover, the policies associated with the plans in his book to rebuild the Japanese archipelago began to be pursued in this period and continue to be a lasting legacy of his administration today.

Tanaka's plans all required massive investments of funds, and economic growth would have to be maintained to generate government revenue to pay for the schemes. Some of the spending could be financed by government borrowing, but the Ministry of Finance was traditionally opposed to deficit financing. It also assumed that annual growth rates of GNP would continue to be high – perhaps not the 11 per cent of the preceding decade but still well above 5 per cent. It also assumed that the infrastructure and other programmes in the Tanaka programme would be smoothly implemented to support continued growth.

When Tanaka became Prime Minister in the summer of 1972, he ordered the Economic Planning Agency (EPA) to create a long-term economic plan consistent with his domestic policy vision. As Lincoln points out:

> As a whole, the plan was a very liberal document, endorsing a wide range of social programs, including increased spending on housing, expanded public park lands, more resources for home care and

community care of the elderly and seriously handicapped, increased spending on medical facilities, and the institution of a five-day work week. The authors of the plan did acknowledge that to achieve these goals increased government deficits would be necessary. With a modest slowdown in private sector investment, they predicted that government expenditures on social programs would cause a six trillion yen deficit by fiscal year 1977, or approximately 22 billion dollars at average 1973 exchange rates . . . Continued rapid growth would allow the government to make these new or expanded expenditures without going too far into debt because tax revenues would rise rapidly. Finally, growth would absorb resources at home, keeping the current account surplus under control so that Japan would not get into trouble with its trading partners.[22]

The enthusiasm and optimism of the Economic Planning Agency was understandable, as Tanaka's vision of the new Japan gave the officials in the agency a new sense of purpose, and many benefited directly from the expansion of new government agencies, such as the Land Agency, and quasi-governmental organisations, such as the National Institute for Research Advancement, which not only promoted Tanaka's ideas but provided new and lucrative career opportunities for Tanaka's allies in the bureaucracy. There is little doubt that the political will behind his vision was crucial to the rapid implementation of his policy initiatives, but he was also successful in getting the bureaucracy to do his bidding as a result of years of cultivation of key members of the ministries. He flattered them, argued with them, impressed them, promoted them, persuaded them, and rewarded them. His ability to win the agreement of the Ministry of Finance bureaucrats to large-scale government deficit spending was most impressive.

Local governments and MPs were also enthusiastic about the Tanaka programme. It was the culmination of several pieces of legislation under which 'all of Japan was classified into either Departure Promotion Areas, for regions already overcrowded and overenlarged, or Relocation Reception Areas, for regions which should attract new industries. Relocation Areas by the 1980s covered 86.5 per cent of Japan.'[23] That the schemes were milked for patronage opportunities is evidenced by the fact that relocations disproportionately benefited Tanaka and his supporters. 'For example, there is no clear economic reason for locating a major mechatronics research center, Japan's International University and several new high technology ventures in Nagaoka, a small town two hundred miles from Tokyo' in

Tanaka's district.[24] Similarly, Tanaka's vision of high-speed bullet trains networking Japan resulted in a minor branch to his district being completed prior to links with major cities through the country.

Of course, all these new programmes cost money, and, as Curtis points out, the amounts were significant:

> Under Tanaka's leadership the government's general accounts budget for fiscal year 1973 provided for a 25 per cent increase over the previous year's budget, the largest year-to-year increase in the post-war period. Public works expenditures jumped 32 per cent, social welfare was up an equally impressive 29 per cent. And Tanaka celebrated welfare's birthday and the government's new enlarged spending by giving the electorate a two-trillion-yen tax cut. No country has moved more quickly to embrace so broad a range of new and expanded government-sponsored social welfare programs than did Japan in the early seventies.[25]

Strangely enough, few political scientists seem willing to attribute a major role to Tanaka in this sudden shift to ambitious spending plans in the areas of welfare and regional development, as well as the new responsiveness to issues such as pollution control. Instead, there is a tendency to stress structural or political causes. It is argued that Japan's economy had grown so rapidly that the demand for change was inevitable and the LDP was naturally responsive to these demands. Yet it is unmistakable that the shift in policy was associated with Tanaka: it did not happen before Tanaka, nor did such dramatic initiatives occur after Tanaka. This is not to suggest a 'great man' view of history, but to ignore the man, what he stood for and how he pursued these goals is to omit a significant part of the explanation for the changes that were made.

A typical attribution of such changes to generic causes can be found in Kato:

> By the 1960s, Japanese welfare expenditures were about half those of the United States and about a third of those of former West Germany in terms of the GDP share. At the beginning of the 1970s, public demand for an improved quality of life replaced the demand for economic growth, which had been the government's first priority in the 1960s; social welfare and environmental pollution issues had also become major public concerns. The predominant LDP, which had responded to these new demands more slowly than the opposition parties, began to suffer from losses in both its popular support

and numerical strength in the Diet. Once the LDP government perceived this political crisis, it became an important reason for the subsequent expansion of welfare programs. Around the beginning of 1973, immediately before the Japanese economy began to be influenced by the recession that resulted from the oil price shock, the government pushed for an active fiscal policy in the supplementary budget of the 1972 fiscal year and the budget of the 1973 fiscal year.[26]

Even Kato recognises Tanaka's role in this:

> This budget expansion, represented by the enormous 1973 budget of 14.28 trillion yen (52.46 billion dollars at 1 dollar = 272.2 yen) – up 24.6 per cent even from the 1972 anti-recession budget – was moved ahead by Prime Minister Kakuei Tanaka (July 1972 to December 1974). A 30 per cent increase in social security expenditures from the previous year caused the 1973 fiscal year to be labelled 'the first year of the age of social welfare.' The 32.2 per cent increase in public works reflected Prime Minister Tanaka's 'Plan for Remodelling the Japanese Archipelago' (*Nihon Retto Kaizoron*) to develop and industrialize, especially the rural areas, by distributing public money.[27]

However, Kato returns to a very unpersuasive structural argument concerning the reasons for the Ministry of Finance's conversion to a positive fiscal policy which in reality was due to Tanaka's cultivation as much as any other factor:

> The MOF's acceptance and cooperation with the prime minister's expansive fiscal orientation during this period were different from its fiscal conservatism before and after it. The fiscal bureaucrats had a special reason to cooperate: they wanted to decrease a surplus in the international account by increasing domestic demands [sic]. This surplus had brought international pressure for re-evaluation of the yen since the declaration by the US President Nixon to suspend the convertibility of gold ('dollar shock') in August 1971. A majority of Japanese policymakers believed that decreased international competitiveness would be caused by a change in the exchange rate from 360 yen to 308 yen per dollar in December 1971.[28]

It is unlikely, however, that Fukuda, the alternative to Tanaka, would have been so keen to upset fiscal orthodoxy. Moreover, as subsequent events would show, the window of opportunity for such policies was very small. The point is not that without Tanaka there would have been no welfare state expansion in Japan, but that the changes would have been smaller, more fitful and less deeply entrenched in the Japanese political system. Moreover, it was not only Tanaka, but also his senior faction members who contributed to his policy initiatives. Tomisaburo Hashimoto was a Tanaka faction member with a passion for welfare reform which derived from his experiences with a handicap. Tanaka attracted such people to his faction because the politics of welfare and assistance was consistent with Tanaka's approach to his constituency and accommodation with the opposition. Indeed, it would help many of the LDP's core constituents and undermine the opposition by using opposition policies against their proponents.

The side payments to small business show a similar logic, though the benefits were much more targeted to key LDP constituencies. Calder has argued that the small business programmes begun during the Tanaka administration were a direct reaction to the gains made by the Communist Party in urban areas in the 1972 general election. Notwithstanding the rhetoric of paranoid right-wing politicians, the threat to the LDP from a party which gained the support of less than 10 per cent of the electorate was minimal.[29] It is true that the no-collateral loan programme, which the government adopted and which caused central government small business expenditure to rise 29 per cent in the period 1973–4 alone, had been pioneered by left-wing local governments in major cities, but the benefits of the Tanaka plan were spread throughout Japan to the constituents upon whom the LDP had always relied as well as to new areas. Even more significant was the Large Scale Retail Store Law of 1973 which controlled the expansion of chain stores. It gave protection to the very clients that Tanaka had always served and still allowed chain stores to expand so long as they could buy off the opposition of local small businesses.

There was a parallel for both the welfare and small business initiatives in the so-called Pollution Parliament of 1970 when Japan moved quickly to implement environmental legislation after years of complacency. Tanaka had been party secretary at the time and must have realised the popularity of such an initiative. He borrowed much of the rhetoric of the environmental initiative of 1970 for his own social spending campaign: 1970 had been termed Pollution Year One so Tanaka declared 1973 Welfare Year One; the Pollution Parliament was followed by the Welfare Parliament.

Pollution control policy was not all posturing, however. Tanaka was an enthusiastic supporter of pollution control legislation, perhaps due to close experience with pollution in the Showa Denko pollution case in Niigata which involved mercury poisoning which produced horrifying illness and birth defects. A man such as Tanaka who truly seemed to love his native Niigata could not help but be moved to action by this issue. Accordingly, when he became Prime Minister, Tanaka appointed activist managers to the newly created Environmental Agency:

> Dr. Buichi Oishi, Prime Minister Kakuei Tanaka's first appointee to the post of director-general of the Environmental Agency, was an energetic, outspoken environmental crusader. It is quite likely that just as he won the affection of the general public for taking strong stands on environmental questions, he transmitted a sense of purpose and enthusiasm to the transferred bureaucrats under him.[30]

Oishi's successor, also appointed by Tanaka, was Takeo Miki, another committed director-general who was uncompromising in his efforts to enforce environmental regulations strictly even after the oil crisis in 1973.

Tanaka gave Japan a good strong start to environmental legislation which came under sustained attack after he left office. After the oil crisis and the end of the Tanaka administration, business resistance to pollution controls increased and progress on the issue slowed noticeably. Once again, if this window of opportunity had been squandered by a cautious prime minister who had moved more slowly in implementing regulations, then substantially less progress would have been made.

It is true that environmental activists were largely appalled by the Tanaka scheme to disperse industry and housing throughout Japan.[31] Still, most Japanese, and especially rural Japanese in constituencies such as Tanaka's, overwhelmingly supported further economic development in their regions if it meant jobs and economic opportunities. Even when the development projects came and they failed to deliver, it only whetted local appetites for more. So, one cannot say that Tanaka, most of the LDP and its supporters were ardent environmentalists; for them economic development was the first priority despite any commitment to pollution control.

Special action was always taken to diffuse environmental opposition to industrial development. As Samuels points out in the case of nuclear power:

Prime Minister Tanaka, avidly pro-nuclear and notoriously pro-pork barrel, in 1974 set up a special account derived from electricity taxes for the siting of nuclear power plants. The amount available more than doubled between 1976 and 1983. In 1977 alone it was greater than the total amount spent in the two decades between 1956 and 1975. In 1983, these funds, euphemistically called 'cooperation money' and obviously designed to coopt residential opposition through large expenditures on public works, amounted to 14 per cent of the nation's nuclear power budget.[32]

Tanaka's key goal was to diffuse opposition, whether by concessions or bribery, in order to ensure that development goals were maintained.

. . .

CONCLUSION

Those who argue that the LDP was responsive and flexible in dealing with the problems created by high-speed growth usually point to Tanaka's achievements which set the stage for later developments. What is less emphasised is the fact that this responsiveness was intimately connected to Tanaka's populist style of politics and the process of cultivating and co-opting support. While the intention was to solve the problems facing Japan, it is also notable that the methods did not preclude substantial benefits, in effect massive side-payments, to all and sundry, but mainly to LDP constituencies.

Tanaka's foreign policy successes were the most lasting. He improved relations with China, made progress with the Soviets, and gave Japan an independent voice in foreign affairs. Any one of these initiatives could be explained by the demands of the time but only Tanaka had the strength to pursue all these policies with a depth of conviction which overcame the rigid thinking of Foreign Ministry officials and foreign governments. His initiatives are central to an understanding of postwar Japanese foreign policy.

Tanaka's domestic policy initiatives were also important. Welfare, land policy, pollution policy and small business policy are among the many issues his short but energetic administration managed to confront, though as we will see, these new policies often created as many problems as they solved. It might seem a mystery, given his promising start, why Tanaka fell from power so quickly afterwards.

However, his methods of gaining power and transforming Japan contained the seeds of his own destruction. Moreover, the negative consequences of his demise would be as powerful and as lingering as the positive benefits of his brief stint in power.

. . .

NOTES AND REFERENCES

1 Yoh Mizuki, *Tanaka Kakuei: Sono Kyozen to Kyoaku* [Kakuei Tanaka: His Greatness and Wickedness] (1998), p. 142.
2 *Ibid.*, p. 170.
3 *Ibid.*, pp. 168–9.
4 *Ibid.*, pp. 171–7.
5 I.M. Destler, Haruhiko Fukui, and Hideo Sato, *The Textile Wrangle: Conflict in Japanese–American Relations, 1969–1971* (Ithaca, NY, 1979), pp. 297–305.
6 Mizuki, *Tanaka Kakuei*, p. 186.
7 *Ibid.*, pp. 190–2.
8 Herbert Passin, 'Intellectuals in the Decision-making Process', in Ezra F. Vogel (ed.), *Modern Japanese Organization and Decision-making* (Berkeley, CA, 1975), p. 281.
9 Gerald L. Curtis, 'Big Business and Political Influence', in *ibid.*, p. 40.
10 *Ibid.*, p. 40n.
11 Takashi Endou, *Tanaka Makiko: Chichi kara Musume e no Yuigon* [Makiko Tanaka: Last Testament of a Father to his Daughter] (1994), p. 79.
12 Yoshihisa Hara, *Kishi Nobusuke: Kensei no Seijika* [Nobusuke Kishi: A Politician of Authority] (1995), p. 236.
13 Haruhiko Fukui, 'Tanaka goes to Peking', in T.J. Pempel (ed.), *Policymaking in Contemporary Japan* (Ithaca, NY, 1977), pp. 78–84.
14 Akiko Sato, *Watakushi no Tanaka Kakuei Nikki* [My Kakuei Tanaka Diary] (1994), pp. 105–6.
15 Chae-Jin Lee, *Japan Faces China* (Washington, DC, 1976), p. 122.
16 *Ibid.*, p. 125.
17 Kazuo Chiba, 'Japan and the Middle East in the 1970s and early 1980s', in K. Sugihara and J.A. Allan (eds), *Japan in the Contemporary Middle East* (London, 1993), p. 148; Shigezo Hayasaka, *Hayasaka Shigezo no Tanaka Kakuei Kaisoryoku* [Shigezo Hayasaka's Kakuei Tanaka Memoir] (1987), pp. 234–44.
18 Shiro Nagano, *Tanaka Seiken 886 Hi* [The Tanaka Administration: 886 Days] (1982), p. 213.
19 Akifumi Ikeda, 'Japanese relations with Israel', in Sugihara and Allan (eds), *Japan in the Contemporary Middle East*, p. 158.
20 *Ibid.*, p. 180, n. 6.

21 Gerald Curtis, *The Japanese Way of Politics* (New York, 1988), p. 64.

22 Edward Lincoln, *Japan: Facing Economic Maturity* (Washington, DC, 1988), pp. 22–4.

23 Kent Calder, *Crisis and Compensation: Public Policy and Political Stability in Japan, 1949–1986* (Princeton, NJ, 1988), p. 308.

24 *Ibid.*, p. 309.

25 Curtis, *The Japanese Way of Politics*, p. 64.

26 Junko Kato, *The Problem of Bureaucratic Rationality: Tax Politics in Japan* (Princeton, NJ, 1994), p. 114.

27 *Ibid.*

28 *Ibid.*, pp. 114–15.

29 Calder, *Crisis and Compensation*, p. 346.

30 Margaret McKean, 'Pollution and Policymaking', in Pempel (ed.), *Policymaking in Contemporary Japan*, pp. 230–1.

31 Survey quoted in Margaret McKean, *Environmental Politics and Citizen Politics in Japan* (Berkeley, CA, 1981), pp. 134–5, esp. n. 4.

32 Richard Samuels, *The Business of the Japanese State* (Ithaca, NY, 1987), p. 246.

Chapter 6

PROLONGED FALL

Tanaka fell from office relatively quickly due to a decline in popularity as a result of economic crisis and revelation of his questionable financial dealings, both of which his opponents used to undermine his government. Despite his removal, Tanaka's efforts to maintain an influence continued to destabilise Japanese politics for over a decade. This process of destabilisation extended beyond LDP factional intrigue to the involvement of opposition parties. Though it was clear toward the end of the process that Tanaka had lost, even his enemies were wary of writing him off too soon. Indeed, this final period of Tanaka dominance shaped his successors, the LDP and Japan for years after his fall from office.

While Tanaka might have enjoyed a degree of foreign policy success, his domestic political standing quickly deteriorated. The first sign of vulnerability came in the 1972 general election. Tanaka had promised the leader of the *Komeito*, among others, that he would not seek an election early in his term, but the Socialists were pushing for an early election and many MPs in Tanaka's own party were actively campaigning in anticipation of an early election. Tanaka found it difficult to resist the need to get the election out of the way to ensure the smooth running of parliament in the following year.[1] Unfortunately for the LDP, the election was a disaster.

The total LDP vote fell by only 1 per cent, but the number of seats they captured fell from 297 before the election to only 271 – the worst result for the party since it was formed. At the same time, the number of Socialist seats rose from 87 to 108 and the Communists' tally more than doubled from 14 to 38. On the other hand, the *Komeito* – who had believed Tanaka's word and had been unprepared for the election – fell 47 to 29 seats, and the moderate Democratic

Socialists also declined from 29 to only 19 seats. The overall percentage of LDP votes had not fallen because powerful LDP MPs such as Tanaka held or increased their vote totals in rural Japan, but in urban Japan the Socialists and Communists gained at the expense of parties further to their right, including the LDP.

Immediately after the election, Tanaka made another serious miscalculation when he proposed a single-member constituency system of election for the powerful Lower House of the Japanese parliament. It was not a new idea. Hatoyama had proposed a similar scheme during his brief tenure of office. The problem was that it hit directly at the seats of too many sitting MPs. Under the multi-member constituency system, between three and five MPs were elected in most districts, with at least one opposition MP winning a seat in even the staunchest of LDP strongholds, such as Tanaka's own home district. A single-member constituency proposal would eliminate many seats held by the opposition who generally only captured a minority of a district even in urban areas, but urban LDP MPs would find it impossible to gain a seat. Even in rural areas where more than one LDP MP ran per district, many seats would be uncertain at best and, depending on the district lines, would lead to the potential defeat of many in the LDP itself. Thus, the plan faltered due to opposition from both inside and outside the LDP. Tanaka had not only cluttered his political agenda with an unpopular policy initiative, but he had also alienated many of the MPs who brought him to power in the first place.

This failure was followed by a surprise attack on Tanaka by the far right. It was a surprise because, in terms of style and personal connections, Tanaka was a man of the right, and prominent right-wingers, such as the faction leader Ichiro Nakagawa, had even supported Tanaka in the presidential election. However, Tanaka's moves to improve relations with the communist People's Republic of China upset those right-wing MPs who wanted to maintain Japan's close links with the anti-communist Republic of China on Taiwan. Tanaka had skilfully managed to keep most of the senior LDP MPs who held these views in check, but the first protests came not from them, but from a younger group of MPs led by Nakagawa.

The emergence of the *Seirankai*, or Blue Storm Society, has been attributed to the inability of Tanaka to incorporate younger MPs into his government. He believed that his administration would be a long one so he felt that less experienced party MPs could wait for their turn in office.[2] The members of the *Seirankai*, however, purported to have loftier motives. They argued that Japan was in need of spiritual renewal. Political corruption was rife and they wanted to reinvigorate Japan through a stronger focus on security issues, education reform and defence of liberty. The members of the group all signed a pledge to each other in their own blood to cement the bond between them. This was classic right-wing behaviour and rhetoric which recalled the nationalist groups of pre-war Japan.

Ironically, it was because this group shared Tanaka's background and political style that they became the vanguard of the attack on his government. None of the members could be said to be part of the Japanese elite. Eight of the group were former bureaucrats, such as the leader Nakagawa, but they had never reached the heights of their profession and left as relatively low-status officials.[3] The background of the remaining members is also telling. For example, Michio Watanabe, another key member, had been a travelling salesman, and Yoshiro Mori was the son of a deeply religious former landlord who gave his land to his tenants even before land reform. At the same time, all the members had a higher level of education than Tanaka, with most having attended university, though not the most prestigious institutions such as Tokyo University. They believed that they would speak for the common man given their backgrounds but that they were better than Tanaka, at least ethically. In itself, this new group was not significant but it gave expression to a sense of growing disillusionment with the Tanaka administration.

.   .   .

ECONOMIC CRISIS

Both the electoral gains made by the left and the sense of crisis on the right were fuelled by clear signs of economic crisis. In part, these were due to events out of Tanaka's control, such as the oil crisis of 1973, but to a large degree, Tanaka's policies exacerbated major economic problems, even if they did not actually create them. His high level of popularity plummeted and he started to lose control of political events. Economic issues were important because although they did not directly bring him down, they were a crucial subtext to the political situation which led to his demise.

Tanaka's plans for a dramatic shift in regional policy had the immediate effect of fuelling a boom in land speculation. Vast rural areas suitable for the relocation of industry suddenly became valuable. In particular, properties near to large government land holdings gained disproportionately in value as development was anticipated. At the same time, urban land prices began to skyrocket. While the overall rise in the cost of land predated the Tanaka administration, prominent cases of speculative booms gave credence to the notion that Tanaka's regional policy was one of the main factors.

In fact, the origins of the land price rise, as well as other economic problems, went deeper. The so-called dollar shock meant the yen was no longer convertible to the dollar at the favourable exchange rate of 360 yen and this had domestic economic repercussions. These problems were compounded by the oil crisis caused by the Arab oil embargo in 1973. In just two months in early 1974, the price of crude oil more than tripled. In response, Tanaka pushed ahead with government spending on high-speed bullet trains and other public works to buoy up the domestic economy and avoid recession.

The combination of a slowing economy and increased spending merely enlarged the government deficit. Lincoln notes:

> The authors of [Tanaka's spending] plan did acknowledge that to achieve these goals increased government deficits would be necessary. With a modest slowdown in private sector investment, they predicted that government expenditures on social programs would cause a six trillion yen deficit by fiscal year 1977, or approximately 22 billion dollars at average 1973 exchange rates. By way of comparison, the actual government deficit in fiscal 1977 was 9.6 trillion yen.[4]

The situation was further exacerbated by serious inflation which had been a problem before the oil crisis. Until 1972, the inflation rate had been around 4–6 per cent on average, but by 1973 it had risen to 11.7 per cent and by 1974 was at 24.5 per cent, with food prices rising as much as 30 per cent on an annual basis. Inflation encouraged panic buying which created a sense of economic chaos. Essentials such as toilet paper were particularly prone to hoarding, with television showing scenes of housewives fighting one another for the last few packages.

In the midst of all these problems, Tanaka's Finance Minister suddenly died. Tanaka desperately needed to restore the confidence of business and the Japanese public, and as a result he decided to appoint Fukuda as Finance Minister. The Fukuda faction had begun to mobilise itself against the Tanaka government, so it made political as well as economic sense to bring Fukuda more firmly into the cabinet.[5] At his first press conference as the new Finance Minister Fukuda reported that Tanaka had given him a free hand to reconsider all policies and make appropriate adjustments, and when asked what this meant for Tanaka's plans to restructure the Japanese archipelago, he replied that the Tanaka plan was Tanaka's alone, and was not government policy.[6] Officially at least, the Tanaka programme had been put on hold.

. . .

REMOVAL FROM POWER

The next test for the government was the 1974 Upper House election. Tanaka was eager to limit the potential damage to the party in a situation where the LDP had seen its electoral support declining for years and the opposition reaching near parity. It was not unlikely that the LDP would lose control of the Upper House. In anticipation of possible defeat, Tanaka spent money frantically. The party was just able to hold on to its majority with 50.4 per cent of the seats, with most of the opposition parties gaining little, except the Communists who rose from 4.5 per cent to 7.9 of the seats in the Upper House. Tanaka had succeeded, but at the price of creating the image of a money-tainted style of politics which few could now ignore.

At this point, Tanaka's Environment Agency Minister, Miki, tendered his resignation. Privately he was disturbed by the cost of the election and wanted to be able to act as a free agent to promote party reform. While Tanaka tried to minimise the significance of Miki's action, the cabinet was further undermined by the resignation of Fukuda, followed by the minor faction leader Shigeru Hori who had been Director General of the Administrative Management Agency. Tanaka duly replaced all three but it was clear that the forces against him within the party were growing. The only hope was that Miki and Fukuda's move would be seen as bitterness over Tanaka's victory over them in the LDP presidential race and a continuation of petty factional politics.

The final big shock to Tanaka, however, came from revelations of his dubious dealings in the past. It is possible that his political enemies assisted in the effort to expose Tanaka's alleged wrong-doing, but the information was systematically dug up by one man, Takashi Tachibana, and merely reinforced public doubts about the Prime Minister. Tachibana's article in the November 1974 issue of the monthly magazine *Bungei Shunju* entitled 'A Study of Kakuei Tanaka – His Financial and Personal Connections' exposed most of Tanaka's questionable activities: his ghost companies, the involvement of friends and relatives in business deals, his spending on his faction and support groups, the land sales and possible use of insider information.

It is significant that the story appeared in the magazine *Bungei Shunju*, a general interest magazine with both fiction and non-fiction features, rather than in the daily newspapers or their associated new magazines. Of course, the major Japanese daily newspapers had reporters covering Tanaka even before he became Prime Minister and knew him well. The problem was that many of the major press bureaux and newspapers had benefited from the sale of government land in prime real estate locations as a direct result of Tanaka's influence. Moreover, the reporters from these new organisations spent hours talking with him both formally at press conferences and informally over glasses of expensive imported whisky at his Meijiro home in Tokyo. They had also heard the stories of shady dealings and questionable practices but it would have been fruitless for them to investigate the allegations even if they had been inclined to do so. As part of the semi-formal reporter groups (*kisha kurabu*) assigned to major politicians, organisations and industries, they were given privileged access to information. Any attempt to dig too deeply, however, would only mean that information would cease to flow as maverick reporters would be excluded from news scoops and informal background information. Besides, most of the allegations were not new.

The business establishment was no doubt largely unsurprised by the revelations of Tanaka practices. While few of the main business players were directly involved with Tanaka himself, most businesses had been engaged in similar dealings. Even so, the allegations of wrongdoing were a convenient pretext for attacks to begin on Tanaka from business leaders. The chairman of the board of Toshiba, Toshio Doko, was selected as the new leader of the main business federation, *Keidanren*, and was particularly outspoken in his criticisms in what seemed part of a larger campaign to put pressure on Tanaka to resign as economic problems multiplied.[7] When members of his own faction began to express doubts, Tanaka finally relented and agreed to resign.

The contest to succeed Tanaka was a three-way one between Fukuda, Ohira and Miki. Ohira had the backing of Tanaka, and based on sheer numbers looked to be likeliest to win another presidential contest. The other factions were not happy with this prospect since it would still leave Tanaka with disproportionate control in the LDP. The party needed a new image. In the end, the LDP vice-president and minor faction leader, Etsusaburo Shiina, forged an agreement to install Miki as Prime Minister. Miki had a reputation as a 'clean' politician, and because his faction was a small one, he was less of a threat to the balance of power in the party than Fukuda or Ohira. The four main faction leaders – Fukuda, Ohira, Miki and Nakasone – agreed to the proposal and Miki replaced Tanaka on 9 December 1974.

. . .

LOCKHEED SCANDAL

Long after Tanaka left office, he remained a power to be reckoned with in the LDP and in Japanese politics as a whole. His efforts in the first year of the Miki administration were aimed primarily at building up his faction and expanding his influence in the ruling party. It was clear that he had not given up hope of regaining power some day, and his earliest political mentors – including Yoshida, Ikeda, Kishi and Sato – had all experienced severe setbacks in their political careers and still gained or regained high political office. As long as he remained leader of his faction, he was a key player and candidate for prime minister.

The problem was that even though the improprieties uncovered in the *Bungei Shunju* article never led to any investigation, let alone legal action against Tanaka, an entirely different set of allegations soon preoccupied him. Once again, these were not revealed in the mainstream press as a result of investigative journalism nor as a result of a police investigation. They were revealed incidentally as a product of United States Senate hearings on corrupt practices which can be viewed as the fallout of the Watergate scandal. It was the Lockheed scandal which this time led to Tanaka's indictment, arrest, trial and conviction. This scandal dogged Tanaka for the rest of his political career and limited his future as a politician to a greater extent than he was willing to acknowledge.

The substance of the allegations was that Tanaka had used his authority as Prime Minister to influence the purchase of Lockheed L-1001 TriStar airbuses by All Nippon Airways (ANA). ANA had already taken an option on the purchase of McDonnell-Douglas's DC-10s, but in August 1972, the vice-president of Lockheed visited Japan and approached Hiro Hiyama, president of the Marubeni Corporation. He also asked Yukio Kodama, an influential figure in gangster and right-wing circles who had been Lockheed's consultant since 1958, to arrange a meeting with Kenji Osano, Tanaka's friend who had earlier bought Tanaka's failing Nihon Denko housing company and benefited from Tanaka's land sales.

As Hertzog notes, 'The crucial event of the scandal took place on 23 August 1972. Accompanied by Toshihara Okubo, Managing Director of Marubeni, Hiyama visited Tanaka at his Meijiro residence. After introducing Okubo, Hiyama had a short conversation with Tanaka . . . Tanaka, upon hearing Hiyama's request, said "*yosha, yosha*".'[8] '*Yosha*' was Tanaka's way of acceding to any request, whether from a constituent or a business leader, without making a firm commitment. After Hiyama decided that 500 million yen would be an appropriate present for Tanaka, a second managing director of Marubeni, Hiroshi Ito, telephoned Toshio Enomoto, one of Tanaka's personal secretaries, who agreed to act as contact man for Tanaka while Okubo would act for Lockheed. Hertzog concludes:

> Between August 1973 and February 1974 [Lockheed's representative in Tokyo] delivered to Ito cardboard boxes stuffed with cash which Ito handed to Toshio Enomoto, Tanaka's secretary, at four different locations . . . Altogether Lockheed seems to have spent 2,634 million yen on promoting the sale of TriStar in Japan. Of this sum, 1.8 billion yen went to Kodama for consulting fees, and Kenji Osano received 54 million yen. The rest was paid to politicians; 500 million yen to Tanaka through Marubeni and an additional 10 million through ANA . . .[9]

In addition, Marubeni made donations to several other politicians, including Susumu Nikaido, LDP General Secretary and senior Tanaka faction member, and Tomisaburo Hashimoto, Minister of Transport, 3 million yen each to Kazutomi Fukunaga (then chairman of the Special LDP Committee on Aviation) and Hideyo Sasaki (former Minister of Transport), and 2 million yen each to Takayuki Sato (then parliamentary Vice-Minister of Transport) and Mutsuki Kato (former parliamentary Vice-Minister of Transport).[10]

The result was not just a problem for Tanaka but for the LDP as a whole. A group of MPs within the party began to doubt whether it could be reformed from within, and were considering quitting the LDP en masse. The origin of the notion of abandoning the LDP may have been the plans of Miki to split the party before his selection as prime minister. Indeed, the threat may have been one of the reasons why the other faction leaders acquiesced in his selection as prime minister. This time, however, five Lower House and six Upper House MPs did resign from the LDP to form the New Liberal Club in protest over the corruption in LDP politics. The LDP needed to distance itself from Tanaka if it was to stop the haemorrhaging of its supporters and MPs.

Tanaka, on the other hand, was desperate to maintain an influence in the party so that he could use his leverage to block the prosecution or at least gain a pardon should his case result in a conviction. However, his influence failed to stop his arrest on 27 July 1976 when two members of the Special Investigation Department of the Tokyo Public Prosecutor's Office appeared at 6:30 in the morning to take Tanaka into custody. After three weeks in jail, Tanaka was indicted for violation of the Foreign Exchange Control Law and for receiving bribes of 500 million yen ($2.1 million). His bail was set at 200 million yen, which he easily paid, and he was released pending trial.

Sixteen people were indicted in total, including officials from Marubeni and ANA as well as Osano and Kodama. As MacDougall points out, there were other politicians implicated but 'it was impossible to indict these "gray officials" under Japanese law, which in a bribery trial requires proof that the defendant actually received the money, that he knew it was a bribe, and that he was in a position of authority to influence the official business of the government'.[11] It is an indication of the seriousness of the scandal that all of those indicted were eventually found guilty, except for Kodama who died of ill health during his trial.

The Lockheed scandal was the first major scandal in Japan for many years. The conspiracy theories put forward by Tanaka supporters which suggest that he was the target of sinister forces plotting his downfall need to be given some consideration. The argument that the origin of the allegations in the US was evidence of an attempt by the American government and/or industry to attack Tanaka for his attempts to establish Japan's independence in foreign policy, especially resource diplomacy, can be refuted easily. After all, Tanaka was no longer Prime Minister and the Senate committee led by Senator Frank Church was hardly a likely tool of the US oil industry or the national security establishment of the US government.

Instead, one must look at the nature of the legal establishment in Japan to understand how circumstances conspired to leave Tanaka defenceless against eager prosecutors and political enemies. Tanaka was unlucky that the scandal was revealed under the administration of his political enemy Miki, and even more so that the Justice Minister at the time was Osamu Inaba, an MP critical of Tanaka. Justice ministers have the power to exempt individuals from prosecution, as most famously occurred when former Prime Minister Sato was saved from disgrace by such an action in the shipbuilding scandal of 1954. On the Lockheed issue, however, Inaba worked closely with a select few officials in the prosecutor's office to keep the investigation beyond the reach of Tanaka's influence.

Yet perhaps the most important circumstance in 1976 was in the attitude of the prosecutor's office itself. The chief prosecutor who had been close to Tanaka, Ichiro Osawa, had resigned the year before the scandal broke, and the new chief prosecutor, Takeshi Fuse, and the new Tokyo district prosecutor, Tsuneo Kamiya, who was directly responsible for the case, were both devoid of political connections.[12] Public prosecutors had been wary in any case of pursuing politicians since 1968 when a well-connected LDP politician took revenge on senior prosecutors by having them transferred and demoted.[13] Until the Lockheed scandal was thrust upon them, therefore, prosecutors in Japan had not vigorously pursued allegations of impropriety involving politicians, and indeed, there had been no major scandals investigated in the period between 1968 and the Lockheed scandal in 1976. In the Lockheed case, however, the prosecutors involved were very careful to avoid the interference of politicians in their pursuit of the scandal to the extent that they even failed to fully inform Prime Minister Miki of their actions out of fear that he might stop them in order to save his administration.[14]

Such fears had a firm grounding because the arrest of Tanaka almost immediately led to the downfall of the Miki government. Miki, true to his 'clean' image, pushed revisions to the Public Office Election and Political Funds Control Laws through parliament to address the deficiencies in Japan's campaign financing arrangements. His efforts, however, merely persuaded the leaders of the main factions that he had to go in order to bring an end to the divisive and damaging debate over corruption in the LDP. Two-thirds of the LDP MPs in parliament signed a petition against him including 14 of his own cabinet ministers. Miki resigned on 21 October 1976 and his successor, Fukuda, took the party into an election in December in which the LDP only maintained its majority by recruiting independents into the party. As a result of the fight to remove Miki, the LDP was at a new low point, but Tanaka's lingering influence would push the party to even greater depths.

. . .

BEHIND THE SCENES

It was in the period following his arrest that the image of Tanaka was formed in the minds of most Japanese. He pottered around his large home in Meijiro in Tokyo wearing a crumpled suit and Japanese wooden clogs, a *haramaki* corset-like sweater wrapped around his beer belly, fanning himself with an *uchiwa* fan. He looked like a typical middle-aged Japanese man, but one with attitude. His protruding lips sipped at the best imported whisky at a time when import duties and distribution networks meant that only domestically produced whisky was available to most Japanese who wanted it. He was also seen out on the golf courses of Japan in a traditional Western golf outfit playing with the country's rich and powerful men. Golf was another expensive luxury which to many was a symbol of success.

Yet despite his success and his failures, Tanaka was the same irrepressible, confident rural politician. He still talked tough but also in a way which communicated an empathy with the common people. This endeared him to the millions of Japanese who bought the books which pronounced his innocence or at least attributed his downfall to sinister forces in the Japanese establishment, or in the US government. 'How to' books claimed to be able to explain his success, and one asked rhetorically: 'Could you too become Tanaka?'[15] For every strong detractor of Tanaka there was at least one supporter.

It is not surprising, therefore, that with his resignation as Prime Minister and subsequent arrest on bribery charges, Tanaka did not fade in political influence. In fact, the peak of Tanaka's political power was precisely in the period between his arrest in 1976 and his conviction in 1983. It was not so much his public popularity, however, as the growing strength of his faction that gave him continuing political power. As Dennis Smith has put it: 'Until the period of Tanaka Kakuei's dominance, most factions were relatively small. One of Tanaka's innovations in the LDP was the creation of a very large faction, having the allegiance of well over 100 members.'[16]

However, it was not just the size of his faction but how he used it that was decisive. Tanaka faction members were ambitious and eager to follow in the footsteps of their leader. While each Tanaka faction MP had strengths in particular areas – such as fundraising, policy expertise, or ability to deal with the opposition – they all pulled together to increase the size and influence of the faction. Tanaka commanded great loyalty among his faction members, but they also knew that his political power would benefit their careers as well, and the skills that he had cultivated in them would be useful to them in the future even after he was gone.

The Tanaka faction was ruthless. It was not above undermining other factions by running its own candidates against rival LDP faction members and even co-operating with the opposition parties to do so. An example is given by Takabatake of co-operation between members of the Tanaka faction and the Japan Socialist Party (JSP) in fighting the rival faction led by Miki Takeo.[17] Tanaka never forgave Miki for resigning and allowing the prosecutor's office to proceed with action against him, and he resolved to fight Miki, including working against Miki's political followers in Miki's home prefecture of Tokushima. Even the local JSP branch was enlisted to work with the Tanaka faction against Miki in his home district. The incentive for the JSP in Tokushima was the prospect of lucrative public works and other benefits for party constituents.

. . .

CIVIL WAR IN THE LDP

Tanaka could not stop Fukuda from assuming the premiership after the fall of Miki, but he exerted all his efforts in undermining Fukuda during his short time in power. Ironically, it was one of the few innovations introduced into the LDP in the wake of the Lockheed scandal that was to be Fukuda's undoing. The party had adopted a party primary system which gave some weight to party members in the leadership selection contest. It was hoped that the involvement of a large number of party members would weaken the hold of factions and democratise the party. However, Tanaka fully embraced the notion of party member participation and went so far as to pay the membership fees for large numbers of party members throughout Japan. Through his faction's extensive organisation, the party member primary system allowed Tanaka to unseat Fukuda and help elect his ally Ohira instead.

At this point, Fukuda fought back. The Ohira administration, like that of Tanaka, was plagued with problems including a second oil crisis in 1978 and then a defeat in the 1979 general election when the LDP again fell short of a majority (though once again independents were persuaded to join the LDP and restore its hold on power), so Fukuda and his allies continually pressured Ohira to resign but he refused. Fukuda then went so far as to seek the support of opposition parties in trying to replace Ohira as Prime Minister, but to no avail because of Tanaka's special relationship with the *Komeito* and others in the opposition. Finally, in May 1980, the Fukuda and Miki factions deliberately absented themselves from a routine no confidence resolution put forward by the opposition. Parliament was forced to dissolve and the LDP faced a new election in June 1980, less than one year since the last. Then, in the midst of the election campaign, Ohira suddenly died.

The result, however, was a surprise victory for the LDP which gained 36 seats and a secure majority, mostly put down to a sympathy vote in reaction to Ohira's death. One of Ohira's senior faction leaders, Zenko Suzuki, was supported as Ohira's successor by both the Tanaka and Fukuda factions – mainly because Suzuki was a weak Prime Minister who could easily be removed. Not surprisingly, Suzuki only lasted for a single two-year term as party leader after which he decided not to run for re-election, partly because he had been undermined by his mismanagement of US–Japan relations but also because he knew he was vulnerable to the rekindling of conflict between Tanaka and Fukuda as potential opponents to his re-election began to emerge, primarily Ichiro Nakagawa who was backed by Fukuda.

The Tanaka faction was poised to keep Suzuki in place, but with his refusal to run, the faction was faced with a dilemma. It was impossible for Tanaka to re-enter power directly with his bribery trial still ongoing, but for the same reason, he needed to assure that any government was not hostile to him. The solution was that Tanaka shifted his support to the relatively small faction leader Yasuhiro Nakasone, who was also endorsed by former Prime Minister Kishi in the Fukuda camp.[18] Tanaka's endorsement, however, suggested that the 'shadow shogun' (*yami shogun*) had created the government and Nakasone's was afterwards dubbed the 'Tanakasone' administration.[19]

.   .   .

FINAL POLITICAL DEMISE

On 12 October 1983, the Tokyo District Court found Tanaka guilty of bribery and sentenced him to four years in prison and a 500 million yen fine. Tanaka remained free pending his appeal. The opposition parties took the opportunity to obstruct parliamentary proceedings in an effort to force an early general election, which they anticipated they might win. Nakasone finally acceded to their demands and an election was held in December 1983. The result was a serious defeat for the LDP. It once again lost its majority which was only barely restored by the recruitment of a handful of independent conservative MPs. In order to achieve a more secure majority, Nakasone was forced to enter into a coalition with the New Liberal Club, composed of MPs who had split the party over Tanaka several years earlier.

For Tanaka, however, the election was not a personal setback. He was elected by the highest ever vote total in his Niigata district with most of his constituents using the opportunity to send a clear message of support for Tanaka to the country at large. Of course, Tanaka had been good to his district. The numbers speak for themselves: 'In 1982, the residents of his prefecture paid an average of $541 in taxes and received per capita public works of $1,644. In contrast, Tokyo residents paid $3,060 for public works of $815.'[20] It is no surprise that they re-elected him by a comfortable margin.

The Tanaka faction also fared relatively well with the loss of only two members, the least of any of the factions.[21] However, the first signs of discontent started to emerge from within Tanaka's own faction. One of his senior faction leaders, Susumu Nikaido, was persuaded to become involved in an attempt by Fukuda to oust Nakasone with the assistance of the moderate opposition parties, namely the Democratic Socialists and the *Komeito*. Tanaka was not consulted about the moves despite the fact that it was Nikaido, his most loyal lieutenant, who was the candidate to be put forward and that his opposition allies, including the *Komeito*, were at the centre of the plan. This was the first hint that Tanaka's influence was slipping.

Then in February 1985, another senior Tanaka faction leader, Noboru Takeshita, created a 'study group' within the Tanaka faction which included most of the faction. Tanaka persuaded most of the initial members to withdraw, but those who remained were some of the key members of the faction – including Shin Kanemaru, Ozawa Ichiro, Seiroku Kajiyama and Keizo Obuchi. These dynamic younger members were dissatisfied with the inability of the faction to put one of their own in power, but Tanaka was furious at their lack of loyalty and respect.

Ten days after the formation of the new group, Tanaka abruptly cancelled a golf date because he was not feeling well. He had been brooding over the betrayal by some of his closest supporters and had started drinking whisky from well before noon. Feeling tired, he took a nap in the afternoon. In the evening when he awoke he went to the toilet but found he could not move his arms and legs as he tried to get up. He gave out a cry. His wife and daughter rushed to him as he collapsed into unconsciousness. The doctor was called and he informed the family that Tanaka had suffered a severe stroke. His daughter Makiko decided to have him admitted secretly to a hospital where his illness could be kept secret for a while at least.

Makiko desperately wanted to protect her father from being used as a political pawn in manoeuvres to gain power. At the same time, she had no choice but to become involved in political confrontation and stratagems to achieve her goal. One of her first actions was to shut down her father's political office and fire the office manager, her father's long-time mistress Akiko Sato. Further, she used her monopoly of control over access to her father to prolong his influence for as long as possible.

Even in illness, Tanaka's influence was undeniable. As Karel van Wolferen has noted:

Few episodes tell more about Tanaka's power than the way the prime minister and nearly all the other important LDP figures rushed to his bedside when, one day in 1983, he was reported to be having breathing difficulties. When in 1985 he suffered the stoke that marked the beginning of his political decline, even Kiichi Miyazawa, long identified with the anti-Tanaka forces, hurried to the hospital; he knew that, at that time, Tanaka's endorsement was still a prerequisite for becoming prime minister.[22]

Yet Tanaka's grip on his faction was slowly slipping. When Nakasone's third term of office was due to expire in September 1987, Nikaido announced that he would run for Prime Minister as the Tanaka faction candidate. Takeshita knew Tanaka had put Nikaido up to it in an attempt to undermine Takeshita's own candidacy so Takeshita and his supporters immediately bolted from the faction. Takeshita's own groundwork had been so thorough that the majority of the Tanaka faction left with him. Only a handful of Tanaka loyalists remained under Nikaido's leadership. After making a deal with other faction leaders, Takeshita became Prime Minister on 6 November 1987. Tanaka's political life was at an end.

· · ·

NOTES AND REFERENCES

1 Shiro Nakano, *Tanaka Seiken: 886 Hi* [The Tanaka Administration: 886 Days] (1982), p. 254.
2 *Ibid.*, pp. 244–7.
3 Takako Kishima, *Political Life in Japan* (Princeton, NJ, 1991), pp. 85–9.
4 Edward Lincoln, *Japan: Facing Economic Maturity* (Washington, DC, 1988), p. 33.
5 Nakano, *Tanaka Seiken*, pp. 286–9.
6 *Ibid.*, p. 326.
7 Gerald Curtis, 'Big Business and Political Influence', in Ezra F. Vogel (ed.), *Modern Japanese Organization and Decision-making* (Berkeley, CA, 1975), pp. 58–9.
8 Peter Hertzog, *Japan's Pseudo-Democracy* (Folkestone, 1993), p. 159.
9 *Ibid.*, p. 161.
10 *Ibid.*
11 Terry MacDougall, 'The Lockheed Scandal and the High Costs of Politics in Japan', in Andrei Markovits and Mark Silverstein (eds), *The Politics of Scandal* (London, 1988), p. 198.
12 Akira Uozumi, *Tokuso Kensatsu* [Special Investigative Prosecutor] (1997), pp. 68–9.
13 Susumu Mukaidani, *Chiken Tokusobu* [Local Prosecutor Special Investigation Division] (1993), pp. 59–62.
14 Tsutomu Hotta, *Kabe o Yabutte Susume: Shiki Rokiido Jiken* [Tear Down the Wall and Advance: A Private Record of the Lockheed Incident] (1999).

15 Osamu Togawa, *Kimi wa Tanaka Kakuei ni Nareru ka* [Can you become Kakuei Tanaka?] (1980); see also Masaharu Inoue, *Tanaka Kakuei was Muzai de aru* [Kakuei Tanaka is Not Guilty] (1985). Additionally, Naoki Komuro produced at least four books in the early 1980s (including two in the year of Tanaka's conviction) defending Tanaka and advocating his tactics and skills in a Kappa Business book series in Japanese.

16 Dennis Smith, *Japan since 1945* (London, 1995), pp. 124–5.

17 Michio Takabatake, *Chiho no Okoku* [Regional Kingdoms] (1986), pp. 149–83.

18 Tarou Maki, *Nakasone wa Nani dattanoka* [What was Nakasone?] (1988), pp. 19–51.

19 This is the central theme of Jacob Schlesinger, *Shadow Shoguns: The Rise and Fall of Japan's Postwar Political Machine* (Stanford, CA, 1999). A *shogun* in Japanese history was a powerful general who usurped power from the emperor and ruled the country; some Japanese commentators have used the term *yami shogun* ('shadow shogun') to describe the backroom politicians who really pull the strings in Japanese politics. Tanaka is the exemplar: some argue that the term was first used to describe his placement of Prime Minister Suzuki in power.

20 J.M. Ramseyer and F. Rosenbluth, *Japan's Political Marketplace* (Cambridge, MA, 1993), pp. 122–3.

21 Masumi Ishikawa, *Sengo Seiji Shi* [Postwar Political History] (1995), p. 157.

22 Karel van Wolferen, *The Enigma of Japanese Power* (London, 1989), pp. 167–8.

Chapter 7

LEGACY

Tanaka became a reclusive figure after his stroke in 1985 and stayed that way until his death in 1993. His appeal against the bribery conviction wound its way through the Japanese court system at the glacial pace that seems to plague most major legal cases in Japan. It was no coincidence that Tanaka faction members had often been justice ministers in the cabinets since the Lockheed case first went to trial and his allies in government and in the bureaucracy continued to use every opportunity to delay justice. His continuing poor health, in particular, became the grounds for delays which meant he died before his appeal was decided.

Tanaka was no doubt seriously ill. He was partially paralysed as a result of the stroke, his face drooping to one side and his speech slurred. Occasionally, a photographer would catch a glimpse of him as his chauffeured limousine raced past, but that was about the extent of Tanaka's public appearances. At the same time, Tanaka's style of politics was as healthy as ever and developed under those he had taught so well. His death in December 1993 came at a symbolic moment as the Liberal Democratic Party had fallen from power as the result of a scandal in which he was indirectly involved. These events marked the end of one era and the beginning of another, but Tanaka's politics lived on beyond his own life.

The peak of Tanaka-style politics came in the 1980s. In the early part of the decade, Tanaka's faction began to be organised into a political machine.[1] Following Tanaka's example, the members of his faction used their knowledge of the bureaucracy and policy-making process to the benefit of themselves, their constituencies and their supporters. The faction was strongest in posts and telecommunications as well as in construction, but they also made a respectable showing in other policy areas as well. The phenomenon, effectively pioneered by Tanaka, was emulated by other factions and given the name *zoku giin* (tribal MPs), with each 'tribe' of MPs cultivating bureaucrats and policy expertise to achieve their ends.[2] For some, this heralded the rise of policy-competent MPs, but more often than not this expertise was focused primarily on milking the bureaucracy for subsidies and projects to benefit local constituencies and favoured business supporters.

Thus, even with Tanaka's demise, the period from 1987 to 1993 saw a continuation if not an expansion of the worst aspects of Tanaka's style of rule. The Takeshita administration's approach to the resolution of political problems and regional development surpassed Tanaka's in the amount of largesse distributed. In one policy initiative, for example, Takeshita simply gave 10 million yen to every local authority in the country for each to use as it saw fit. Policies to promote the development of leisure facilities saw widespread development of resorts, mainly golf courses, which not only scarred large areas of rural Japan environmentally, but also resulted in a speculative boom culminating in an economic bubble. The wealth created by this bubble finally made it possible for many Japanese to adopt a luxurious lifestyle which became well known throughout the world as Japanese bought prime real estate, drove up the prices of Impressionist paintings and buoyed up the French and Italian fashion industries.

In reaction to the legacy of Tanaka's deficit financing, the Ministry of Finance had convinced politicians that a new tax was necessary to pay for further government spending, proposed by Takeshita. The consumption tax, implemented in 1989, was deeply unpopular and continues to be a political issue today.

In addition, other factions began to emulate Tanaka's approach to the raising of political funds by dubious methods, most obviously in the Recruit scandal, in which most faction leaders were implicated. The Recruit Corporation is a major publisher of magazines in Japan which became the basis of a large economic conglomerate. The president of Recruit, Hiromasa Ezoe, was accused in 1988 (and later convicted) of bribing public officials in order to gain access to sensitive public information and influence public procurement. Not only senior civil servants, but also leading politicians, had received shares in Recruit just prior to its flotation on the Tokyo stock exchange, and many of the latter, including Takeshita, had received generous political donations and loans. The Prime Minister was forced to resign when it became known that he had lied over the extent of these gifts (or loans).

The Recruit scandal not only brought down Takeshita's administration, it prevented all other major faction leaders from assuming control of the government in his place. The LDP finally lost control of the Upper House of parliament in the summer of 1989 as the public reacted strongly to both the consumption tax and the Recruit scandal. Nevertheless, the Takeshita faction was still the power behind the government, just as the Tanaka faction had been even after Tanaka's fall from power. They created the government of Toshiki Kaifu in late 1989 and then, when he began to take seriously the issue of political reform, they dumped him in favour of Kiichi Miyazawa in 1991. Two leading members of the Takeshita faction, Shin Kanemaru and Ichiro Ozawa, even began to toy with making deals with the opposition, particularly the *Komeito*, in moves reminiscent of Tanaka's politics. In fact, Ozawa was Tanaka's favourite – many believed that he loved Ozawa as a replacement for his own son who had died as a child. Kanemaru, too, had been a key Tanaka faction leader and had assumed control of Tanaka's lucrative links with the construction industry after Tanaka had to shun the limelight after his 1983 conviction.[3] Ozawa and Kanemaru were the most feared and respected politicians in Japan until 1992.

. . .

THE LONG REACH OF TANAKA'S INFLUENCE

The problem for Kanemaru and Ozawa was that in 1992 they faced a scandal which reached back to Tanaka himself. The scandal began when Nakasone agreed to support Takeshita for the premiership in exchange for Takeshita's promise to deal with the right-wing splinter group, the Imperial People's Party (*Kominto*), which was noisily campaigning against Takeshita. To stop the campaign, Kanemaru and Takeshita sought the help of the former leader of Japan's second largest criminal syndicate, Susumu Ishii, who maintained connections with the extreme right. The contact person for the meeting with Ishii was Hiroyasu Watanabe, the president of the Tokyo subsidary of Sagawa Express, an express delivery company. After talking to Ryumin Oshima, leader of the *Kominto*, Watanabe held a meeting in a Tokyo hotel with Takeshita, Kanemaru and Ozawa, and persuaded Takeshita to make a visit to Tanaka's residence to apologise for his disloyalty to Tanaka. It turned out that Takeshita's betrayal of Tanaka was at the root of the problem with the *Kominto*.

Takeshita did as requested. On 6 October 1987, he appeared at Tanaka's house in Meijiro, and though he was turned away from Tanaka's front gate in the full glare of news cameras, this seemed to satisfy Oshima and the *Kominto*. In exchange, the crime syndicate chief Ishii received $2 billion in loans from Watanabe, most of which was speculated on the stock market but some of which went to the right-wing Oshima, and Sagawa Express suddenly received increased business from Kanemaru's network of supporters in construction and related industries in exchange for facilitating the cessation of hostility. With this obstacle out of the way, Nakasone formally supported Takeshita and made his selection as Prime Minister inevitable.

When this scandal was exposed, it brought down Kanemaru and sidelined Ozawa and Takeshita – that is, Tanaka's style of politics, which he had taught to the three involved, had brought them all down. Their unquestioning recourse to organised crime to solve problems and their use of bribery and patronage to cope with difficulties were Tanaka's trademark. This time, however, Kanemaru was indicted, arrested and imprisoned while Ozawa was forced out of a position of influence in the Takeshita faction. In turn, Takeshita's faction was destroyed by Ozawa as he led a group of defectors from the faction to form another under the nominal leadership of Tsutomu Hata while the Takeshita loyalists remained under his successor, Keizo Obuchi. Tanaka must have been pleased in the final year of his life to see his own betrayer taste the bitterness of betrayal himself.

In the end, however, not only did this scandal bring down Tanaka's former faction followers, but public outrage at the corruption it revealed ultimately caused the LDP to fall from power after 38 years of continuous government. Even in the last year of his life, Tanaka was therefore, at least indirectly, at the root of the most serious setback to face the LDP in the postwar period. His presence had always been a problem for the party, from its disastrous election showings in the 1970s and 1983 to the loss of control of government in June 1993 only months before his death. It was a fitting end.

. . .

TANAKA POLITICS AFTER 1993

The fall of the LDP led to the formation of a coalition government committed to political reform, and just after Tanaka's death, political reform legislation was passed. It reformed the electoral system in an attempt to discourage factions, and changes were made to control campaign contributions. One important change, intended to deal with such situations as the Lockheed, Recruit and Sagawa scandals, in which the politicians implicated had all been able to claim that their secretaries had acted without their knowledge, made politicians liable for the monies accepted by secretaries and immediate family members. Ironically, however, the main pillar of the reform was the introduction of single-member constituencies, one of Tanaka's failed plans, which would be supplemented with some seats chosen by proportional representation.

The anti-LDP coalition, however, was itself a dubious creation. The long-time opposition parties were involved but the Japanese Socialist Party had been as damaged in the 1993 election as the LDP, even if it was the largest party in the coalition. Moreover, the main players were all former Tanaka faction members or Tanaka's old opposition allies. The coalition government was led by Morihiro Hosokawa, a descendant of an ancient noble family but also a former Tanaka faction member. Even though Hosokawa had quit the faction several years before forming his anti-LDP Japan New Party in 1992, he had still been affiliated with a Tanaka-created think tank, the National Institute for Research Advancement, run by a Tanaka protégé. In addition, the main dynamic force in the coalition was a party led by Hata, a former Tanaka faction member, now controlled by Ozawa, Tanaka's favourite. Finally, Ozawa was allied with another major coalition partner, the *Komeito*, a former Tanaka ally.

As if the dubious nature of the political reform legislation and the coalition government were not enough, there were still signs that the Japanese public's fascination with individuals like Tanaka was undiminished. One of the big best-selling books of 1994 was by Koichi Hamada, a former gangster and Tanaka associate. Hamada had declined to run for re-election in 1993 but took up writing a book in which he denounced all the major politicians of Japan for ruining the country. His style was the rough-cut language of gangsters, not unlike the down-to-earth style of Tanaka. Hamada, however, was a self-confessed 'former' member of a well-known crime syndicate and a construction company owner. He came to prominence for his losses of $2 million in Las Vegas on tours between 1972 and 1974 during the Tanaka administration which were sponsored and paid for by Kenji Osana, Tanaka's business associate, who used Lockheed money to cover the losses.[4] Hamada's popular success 20 years later showed that a philosophy of politics by a man like Tanaka still appealed to the Japanese public.

By the summer of 1994, the LDP had managed to get back into power under the leadership of Yohei Kono, one of the former leaders of the New Liberal Club which had split the LDP in 1976 in protest over corruption. Even more surprising was the fact that the LDP had to make a deal with the Japan Socialist Party in order to get back into power, and it was the Socialist leader, Tomiichi Muryama, who led the government. It was an unstable government which faced serious problems, not the least of which was coping with the consequences of the collapse of the economic bubble. Land prices and the stock market fell dramatically as many of Japan's most successful firms found themselves in such deep debt that their very survival was threatened.

One such firm, Yamaichi Securities, the firm that Tanaka had saved in 1965, collapsed in 1997 with the president of the firm bowing deeply in tears as he apologised for the decision to liquidate the firm. The fact that the government did not save Yamaichi in the aftermath of the bursting of the Japanese bubble economy was symbolic of the refusal of the government to save a major financial institution and heralded other major failures. In a sense, it was Tanaka's actions in 1965 which helped to create the mentality which produced the bubble which brought down Yamaichi in 1997. After Tanaka's bailout of the brokerage industry, the myth that the government would never allow a major financial services firm to collapse took firm hold. In the 1980s, this myth led banks and other financial institutions to behave recklessly and expand the Japanese bubble to the extent that it profoundly damaged the Japanese economy for at least a decade.

On the other hand, many aspects of Tanaka's politics have not changed. The LDP still clings to the old methods: factions still intrigue amongst themselves for control of cabinets and cabinet posts, *zoku giin* still influence policy for the benefit of themselves and their supporters, deals are made with the opposition parties to keep the LDP in power – notably with Ozawa's Liberal Party and the *Komeito* in 1999 – and public works spending is seen as the preferred option to deal with the economic crisis facing Japan. Moreover, it has been former Tanaka faction members who have led the party in this period, with Ryutaro Hashimoto as Prime Minister from 1996 to 1998 and Keizo Obuchi from 1998 to 2000.

It is not surprising that Hashimoto and Obuchi have risen to the top. Not only has every government since the early 1970s been controlled by Tanaka or his successors, but the Tanaka faction and his successors are representatives of the new elite in postwar Japan. This new elite is often the second generation of the elite created immediately after the war. They are more educated than their fathers and have experienced a more privileged upbringing. This is particularly true of the second-generation MPs, who are a wide-spread phenomenon in the LDP and prominent in the Tanaka legacy: former Prime Ministers Hata, Hashimoto and Prime Minister Obuchi, the former New Frontier and Liberal Party leader, Ozawa, and Tanaka's own daughter, Makiko, who is currently one of the most popular politicians in Japan.

While it is true that political families are common in all parliamentary democracies, the phenomenon has been remarkable in Japan, with the first generation of postwar politicians with safe seats being replaced in many cases on their retirement or death by their offspring. By 1991 second-generation politicians constituted 35 per cent of all LDP MPs and many of the most powerful members as well.[5] Even more remarkable is the fact that most cases of second-generation politicians have involved later postwar succession (primarily from the 1960s onwards) and only 11 out of 216 cases have seen pre-war or pre-war/postwar succession between generations. The dominance of Japanese politics by second-generation politicians is a phenomenon which only began in the generation after Tanaka was first elected to parliament, and Tanaka played a major role in promoting the trend by encouraging the children of his faction members to run for office themselves.

Makiko is a good case in point. Tanaka was pleased that his daughter followed in his footsteps. Soon after his death, in 1994, Makiko was given a cabinet portfolio – an unprecedented step for the LDP which had never given such a senior post to a first-term MP. She has the appeal of her father but with the rough edges worn down. Her confidence, money, fashion sense and popular appeal make her perhaps the most outstanding member of the new elite. Even if she never becomes Prime Minister like her father – after all, she does not even belong to a faction – she is still her father's most direct legacy. Yet, in a very real sense, his legacy lives on in all LDP and former LDP MPs and the ways they approach policy and power.

This new elite is symbolic of the rise of the common Japanese at large. The postwar economic miracle and the bubble economy – for all their negative consequences – made the common Japanese (if there is such a thing) wealthy, and their children accept this wealth as natural. In the new cut-throat economic environment, new opportunities exist and new inequalities are emerging but the old status hierarchy has gone. The symbolic journey of the common man and woman in postwar Japan is complete, thanks in no small part to the work of Kakuei Tanaka.

.   .   .

NOTES AND REFERENCES

1 Chalmers Johnson, 'Tanaka Kakuei, Structural Corruption and the Advent of Machine Politics', in his *Japan: Who Governs?* (New York, 1995), pp. 208–9.

2 Takashi Inoguchi and Tomoaki Iwai, *Zoku Giin no Kenkyu* [A Study of Tribal Politicians] (1987).

3 Asahi Shimbun Seijibu, *Seikai Saihen* [Reorganisation of the Political World] (1993), p. 91.

4 David E. Kaplan and Alec Dubro, *Yakuza: The Explosive Account of Japan's Criminal Underworld* (New York, 1986), p. 110.

5 Matsuzaki Tetsuhisa, *Nihon gata demokurashi no gyakusetsu* [The Antithesis of Japanese-style Democracy] (1991), pp. 49, 51.

GUIDE TO FURTHER READING

FURTHER READING IN ENGLISH

A general postwar history of Japan can be found in Dennis Smith's *Japan since 1945* (London, 1995). For a broader historical perspective see Ann Waswo, *Modern Japanese Society, 1868–1994* (Oxford, 1996). Richard Storry's *A History of Modern Japan* (London, 1960; rev. edn 1982) is still good for pre-war and immediate postwar Japanese political history.

Gerald Curtis's book on *Election Campaigning Japanese Style* (Tokyo, 1971) is a classic study of electoral organisation in Japan, and in particular the *koenkai* constituency organisation. Curtis has also written a good study which covers the late 1970s and early 1980s well: *The Japanese Way of Politics* (New York, 1987), and has a book on change in Japanese politics in the 1990s, *The Logic of Japanese Politics* (New York, 1999).

Treatment of the darker side of Japanese political life and its connections with organised crime can be found in David Kaplan and Alec Dubro, *Yakuza: The Explosive Account of Japan's Criminal Underworld* (New York, 1986). A very old article by Harry Emerson Wildes, 'Postwar Politics in Japan II: IV. Underground Politics in Postwar Japan', *American Political Science Review*, vol. 42, no. 6 (Dec. 1948) can still be profitably read for an understanding of the gangster–politician relationship in immediate postwar Japan.

Even though there are dozens of books on Tanaka in Japanese and he looms large in most books in Japanese on postwar political history, there is surprisingly little written about him in English, especially considering the number of studies on other aspects of

Japanese politics. Still useful is Chalmers Johnson, 'Tanaka Kakuei, Structural Corruption, and the Advent of Machine Politics in Japan', *Journal of Japanese Studies*, vol. 12, no. 1 (Winter 1986), which can also be found in a collection of his articles entitled *Japan: Who Governs?* (New York, 1995). However, Johnson's article has been superseded by Jacob M. Schlesinger's *Shadow Shoguns: The Rise and Fall of Japan's Postwar Political Machine* (Stanford, CA, 1999). Schlesinger also covers Tanaka's protégés, Takeshita, Kanemaru and Ozawa, but the book is somewhat limited in its treatment of Tanaka, given the focus of the study. A more offbeat study can be found in Takako Kishima, *Political Life in Japan* (Princeton, NJ, 1991).

Of course, material on the Lockheed scandal usually discusses Tanaka extensively: see Peter Hertzog, *Japan's Pseudo-Democracy* (Folkestone, 1993), and Terry MacDougall, 'The Lockheed Scandal and the High Costs of Politics in Japan', in Andrei Markovits and Mark Silverstein (eds), *The Politics of Scandal* (London, 1988). A general treatment of these issues can be found in Richard Mitchell's *Political Bribery in Japan* (Honolulu, HI, 1996).

Studies of particular elections can also give insight into Tanaka's role in postwar Japanese politics, such as Michael Blaker's *Japan at the Polls: The House of Councillors Election of 1974* (Washington, DC, 1976), and Hans Baerwald, 'Japan's December 1983 House of Representatives Election: The Return of Coalition Politics', *Asian Survey*, vol. 24, no. 3 (March 1984).

Tanaka's contribution to Japanese foreign policy is covered tangentially in I.M. Destler *et al.*, *The Textile Wrangle: Conflict in Japanese–American Relations, 1969–1971* (Ithaca, NY, 1979); Haruhiko Fukui, 'Tanaka goes to Peking', in T.J. Pempel (ed.), *Policymaking in Contemporary Japan* (Ithaca, NY, 1977); and Chae-Jin Lee, *Japan Faces China* (Washington, DC, 1976), among others.

A good understanding of Tanaka-style politics can be found in Kent Calder, *Crisis and Compensation: Public Policy and Political Stability in Japan, 1949–1986* (Princeton, NJ, 1988), and Haruhiko Fukui and Shigeko Fukai, 'Pork Barrel Politics, Networks and Local Economic Development in Contemporary Japan', *Asian Survey*, vol. 36, no. 3 (March 1996), though neither gives Tanaka the attention he deserves considering the focus of these studies. A study on the politics of the construction industry, in which Tanaka and his faction have been deeply involved, can be found in Brian Woodall's *Japan Under Construction* (Berkeley, CA, 1996).

· · ·
FURTHER READING IN JAPANESE

Note: All titles are published in Tokyo unless otherwise noted.

One of the best recent biographies of Tanaka in Japanese is Yoh Mizuki, *Tanaka Kakuei: Sono Kyozen to Kyoaku* [Tanaka Kakuei: His Greatness and Wickedness] (1998). A less objective account can be found in Takao Iwami, *Tanaka Kakuei: Seiji no Tensai* [Kakuei Tanaka: Political Genius] (1999). A good overview which places Tanaka in historical context is Toru Hayano, *Tanaka Kakuei to Sengo no 'Seishin'* [Kakuei Tanaka and the 'Spirit' of Postwar Japan] (1995).

Tanaka himself wrote three books, of which his autobiographical *Watakushi no Rirekisho* [My Curriculum Vitae] (1967) is the most outstanding. In addition, the memoirs of numerous politicians invariably discuss their interaction with Tanaka. However, the books by Shigezo Hayasaka, Tanaka's personal secretary, are generally disappointing, including his *Hayasaka Shigezo no Tanaka Kakuei Kaisoroku* [Hayasaka Shigezo's Tanaka Kakuei Memoir] (1987). Much better material is often produced by those based in Tanaka's native Niigata, such as the Niigata Nippo Hodobu (eds), *Tanaka Kakuei, Rongu Guddobai* [Tanaka Kakuei, Long Goodbye] (Niigata, 1995). The best memoir of Tanaka by far is by Tanaka's former constituency secretary and mistress, Akiko Sato: *Watashi no Tanaka Kakuei Nikki* [My Kakuei Tanaka Diary] (1994). One of his more successful faction members, Tsutomu Hata, has produced an interesting study of the Tanaka legacy in *Tanaka Gakko* [The Tanaka School] (1996).

The most interesting studies of Tanaka's support organisation, the Etsuzankai, are still Asahi Shimbun Niigata Shikyoku, *Tanaka Kakuei to Etsuzankai: Shinso no Kozu* [Tanaka Kakuei and the Etsukzankai: The Layout of the Depths] (1982); Kichiya Kobayashi, *Jitsuroku Etsuzankai* [The Etsuzan Association: A True Record] (1982); and Ryuzo Saki, *Etsuzan Tanaka Kakuei* [Tanaka Kakuei of the Etsu Mountains] (1977).

A few of those involved in the prosecution of Tanaka have produced useful memoirs: Tsutomu Hotta , *Kabe o Yabutte Susume: Shiki Rokiido Jiken* [Tear Down the Wall and Advance: A Private Record of the Lockheed Scandal] (1999), and Akira Uozumi, *Tokuso Kensatsu* [Special Investigative Prosecutor] (1997). Susumu Mukaidani's study of Japan's prosecution service is also very informative: *Chiken Tokusobu* [Local Prosecutor Special Investigation Division] (1993). In addition to books on Lockheed, there is a full-length monograph on Tanaka's involvement in the coal scandal in Ryozo Saki, *Tanaka Kakuei no Fukei: Sengo Shoki Tanko Giwaku* [Tanaka Kakuei's Background: The Early Postwar Coal Control Scandal] (1983).

Takashi Tachibana's *Tanaka Kakuei Kenkyu: Zenkiroku* [Research on Tanaka Kakuei: The Full Record] 2 vols. (1982) covers all the scandals in considerable detail. In fact, Tachibana wrote several books on Tanaka and conducted something of a crusade against him until Tanaka's death in 1993. *Zenkiroku* has achieved classic status and is a must-read in Japanese.

There is a sound study of Tanaka's brief stint as Prime Minister in Shiro Nakano, *Tanaka Seiken: 886 Hi* [Tanaka Administration: 886 Days] (1983). The pernicious influence of Tanaka behind the scenes after his resignation as Prime Minister has been ably documented by several writers. Among the most detailed are the books by Toichi Suzuki including *Nagata-cho no Anto* [Secret Struggles in Nagata-cho] 6 vols. (1978–87). The imagery of the treachery of Japan's warring states period has been used to characterise Tanaka's tactics, including the influential work by Masaya Ito, *Jiminto Sengoku Shi* [History of the Warring States LDP] (1982), and Keiichiro Nakamura's *Tanaka Kakuei Sengoku Shi* [History of the Kakuei Tanaka Warring States] (1985).

Several books on Tanaka's daughter Makiko have appeared in recent years, both critical and supportive. One of the earliest and most informative is Takashi Endo, *Tanaka Makiko: Chichi kara Musume e no Yuigon* [Makiko Tanaka: Last Testament of a Father to his Daughter] (1994). Makiko herself has published a book which contains much autobiographical material providing a further insight into Tanaka as a father and husband: *Jikan no sugiyuki mama ni* [Just Passing the Time] (1994).

INDEX